Susan Paul has written *Your Story Matters* to help those who hunger for a deeper inner life to bridge the gap between things and spirit. I recommend it to anyone who is seeking a greater sense of personal identity in a very cold, impersonal world.
Book Review by JOHN HUNTER, Editor, The Columbia River Observer, Tri-Cities, Washington

Since I've been journaling for the last eight months, it's made such a difference in my life. When I began, it was just an act of 'venting,' but it has become a daily talk to God. Your book has been a great help—I'm even beginning to put together a poem every now and then!
DEANNA NELSON, Artist, Shafter, California

Your book is a worthwhile contribution to those of us who would never, on our own, dare to write or even feel that putting our own words on paper had merit. Reading your book again launched another salvo against defeatist thinking about writing. Thank you.
MAUDINE FEE, Bible Teacher, Speaker, Vancouver, B.C.

My son suggested your book on journaling and writing. . . it has already helped me in sharing an idea with my daughter. . . I look forward to many more insights.
GWEN M. STAVELEY, Speaker, Missionary with MAF, Kent, England

Your encouragement to write a family history is wonderful. I did get my mother to write her memoirs . . . I cherish her child-hood experiences and early family life. It's so important in this technological era to know about life at another pace. CHUCK and MARTHA WHEELER, Authors, Affirming the Darkness, Columbus, Ohio

*Your Story Matters* will be helpful to a generation which desper-ately needs to slow down and reflect on what is of value.
JEAN A. FLEMING, Author, A Mother's Heart and A Homesick Heart, Colorado Springs, Colorado

Susan Paul's beautifully turned-out book is filled with guide-lines for writing, plus samples from writing greats such as G.K. Chesterton, Emily Dickinson, C.S. Lewis, and many others who are not 'big names.' If you have any interest in writing, you're sure to love this book.

Book Review by MITCH FINLEY, Author, Whispers of Love: Encounters with Deceased Relatives and Friends, Spokane, Washington

I've been journaling for twenty-two years and have just finished your book. My story has always mattered to me, but I never thought about it mattering to someone else. I'm going to get out the manuscript for my book and read through it to see what's left to be done. Thank you, thank you!

KATHY BOWERS, Teacher, Kailua, Hawaii

The point you made about friends "here and now" compared with friends "there and now" spoke volumes to me. I have read your book several times, not because it's difficult to understand, but because I want what it says to become a part of me.

PEGGY ANN FOWLER, Homemaker, Kent, Washington

*Your Story Matters* comes for me at a critical time in my life and has been pivotal for me. It is healing for me to think about how my story matters and it has given me new energy for ministry and relationships.

JULIE NELSON LAHMEYER, Nurse, Pastor's wife, Auburn Washington

Your book is hope-giving, with love and courage. Thank you for writing it.

LOUISE HICKMAN, Bakersfield, California

It has been exciting to read your book—even a second time! I am encouraged to be more intentional in getting things written down. Your practical suggestions will be helpful to me.

MAUREEN GWINN, Pastor's wife, Seattle, Washington

Congratulations on your book. The outside is elegant, and the inside, which I gobbled up, is as sharp and to the point as you!

MARIELLE GÉRARD, Benefits Coordinator, Schlumberger International, Paris, France

# YOUR STORY MATTERS

## Introducing the Pleasures of Personal Writing

# Susan Paul

## Inner Edge Publishing

Cover design by Marcie Jacques
Jacques Design
1822 Hummingbird Court, Richland, Washington 99352

Editing by Glenda Schlahta
1518 Rimrock , Richland, Washington 99352

Printing by Press Craft, Inc.
Cover Layout by White Stone Communications, Inc.
1207 South Tenth Street, Pasco, Washington 99301

**Your Story Matters**  Copyright ©1997 Susan I. Paul

Inner Edge Publishing
2221 Benton Avenue
Richland, Washington 99352

ISBN 0-7394-0197-1

*Dedicated to*
*the memory of my beloved brother*

**John Steven Bert**

*June 19, 1962 – February 26, 1992*

*whose story deserves to be written*

# Contents

Preface                                          9

Introduction                                     15

Foundations                                      21

Journaling                                       39

Poetry and Prose                                 67

Story Writing                                    93

Personal and Family History Writing             107

Letter Writing                                  123

End Notes                                        146

Acknowledgments                                 148

Glossary                                        151

Select Bibliography                             154

# Preface

# Third Edition, 1997

All men matter. You matter. I matter.
It's the hardest thing in theology to believe.

G.K. Chesterton
*The Father Brown Omnibus*

Since the first and second editions, I have received numerous letters that have more deeply impressed upon me the need for the messages of this book. Psychologists, mothers with children of various ages, teachers, professors, students, and friends have moved me to print *Your Story Matters* again, with slight revisions. There is more than one way to write your story and there are many people with stories that are waiting to be written!

Many of us hunger for a deeper inner life, a more certain sense of our own identity, and a more personal experience of the spiritual dimension of life. I find this to be universally true and particularly relevant to American culture today. Even among Christians, who have the theology that singularly proclaims the dignity, reclaims the uniqueness and claims eternity for the personality of every person, we find it astounding that we matter. How much more so for those that view the world without hope!

*Your Story Matters* addresses this hunger by showing how writing your story can satisfy your own appetite and nourish others' as well. It presents a smorgasbord of illustrations in a variety of genres, and portions of my own story. If you struggle to believe that you matter or that your life story matters, read on! This book is for you. If you want to write, this book is also for you.

Made in God's image ("a little higher than the angels" the Bible says) *you* are unique. No one else has your fingerprints or DNA code, and no one else has your story.

I write from a Christian perspective because Jesus Christ's story makes sense out of all our stories. No matter what those stories may include, nothing can cancel the love of the seeking God who made us. Christ has bridged the sin chasm that separates us from the Author of Life.

Many of my readers do not share this faith, I realize. The messages of this book are relevant and beneficial, I believe, to all who are interested in writing, regardless of faith orientation, because a large part of the understanding and significance we all seek is bound up in our stories. Valuing them enough to write them is a way toward more focused self-understanding and richer enjoyment of life, whether or not we yet know the Author of our lives.

I dearly hope that this book will inspire you to write. Certainly, I dare hope your interest in the Author of Life might also be inspired. You will find in this book that writing about your life, your thoughts and feelings, your dreams and hopes will help you know yourself better and discover new meaning in your story.

Whether you are a potential writer, a beginning writer, or a "closet writer," I pray this book will encourage you to understand yourself more deeply, value your own story, and preserve it in some way for your children, friends and future generations.

I have enjoyed the pleasures of personal writing for over thirty years. Now I am eager to relate some of these pleasures to you. May they be food for your soul, courage for your heart, and a delight to your mind!

Susan Paul

# Second Edition, 1995

The occasion for the writing of this book was a Writer's Workshop at the West Side Church Women's Retreat, "Expressions of Faith, Lifting Hearts in Celebration to God," February, 1995, in Richland, Washington.

The purpose of the retreat was to bring together women of faith and of all ages to worship and to discover how to use various arts to honor and celebrate God. The day long retreat included artistic workshops (Laughter, Drama, Signing, Music, Writing, Dance, and Visual Arts), along with worship and fellowship over a meal. We hoped to convey that worship is a lifestyle, not an hour on Sundays, and that worship of Jesus Christ can be a refreshing, creative and personally freeing experience. All arts can be a means to revere Him, whether privately or corporately.

The first edition addressed women because of the occasion, but its contents were never for women only.

The need for the book was simple. There was not one book available to use as a basic introduction to all the genres of writing that I wanted to introduce for the expression of personality and faith. I considered using different books to introduce each genre, but limited time and budget prevented this. Even still, there was nothing available in the local bookstores, the library or the various catalogs I researched, on the art of writing poetry nor on the art of letter writing that specifically addressed a person of faith—nor that emphasized the importance of each person's story!

Therefore, I wrote a brief introductory handbook for my workshops, which focused largely on journaling, but also introduced other major forms of creative personal writing as a means of expressing story and faith.

The handbook was inspirational and by no means exhaustive. I am a student of all the forms of writing introduced, and wrote from my experience and research.

I do encourage my readers to *read widely*. There is a wealth of books available to expose you to every kind of writing. Read the books by successful authors that suggest *how to write* in the genre of your choice. Some of these that I have found helpful are mentioned in the body of this work. Others are in the bibliography.

This is a basic principle for all writing: *you must read to write*. Not only is it helpful to read about writing, but it is essential to read within the genres of writing you desire to try. It is virtually impossible to get the feel of a metered verse and write one if you have not read many. Read out loud—you will hear the music of the poetry and see the action of the story more vividly. There are some books available that help explain how to read poetry, or how to tell stories. They will prove especially valuable to those with little exposure to these arts.

However, reading about how to do something or how to understand it is no substitute for jumping into it, any more than reading books on how to swim is a substitute for jumping into the pool and actually swimming.

Another basic principle of writing is this: *what you most enjoy reading may be what you will most enjoy writing*. For example, if you have been "addicted" to a particular kind of novel, you may find that you will enjoy trying your own hand at it. If you have found yourself wishing a story had a different ending, or that a scene or a dialogue was different, your imagination has given you clues that you might enjoy playing with this genre.

Finally, before proceeding, I thank all my contributors for helping me illustrate the point of this handbook: that *you, your story and your journey with God matter.* There seemed to me no better way to illustrate this conviction than to ask some special friends and family members—people whose lives and journeys matter to me—to contribute a few of their creative writings for your inspiration.

Susan Paul

# Introduction

Some writers confuse authenticity,
which they ought always to aim at, with originality,
which they should never bother about.

W.H. Auden
*The Dyer's Hand*

The purpose of this book is to encourage you to value your own story through writing. What you can uniquely write will benefit you and bless others, because you matter and your story matters!

Several genres of creative writing are introduced: journaling, poetry and prose, story writing, personal and family history writing, and letter writing. I hope to build your confidence and freedom to write by persuading you to explore and employ one or more of these genres.

There are other forms of creative writing as well (e.g. technical writing and script writing), but I have little or no experience with them. Journaling, poetry writing, story writing and letter writing are all personal art forms that I know by experience can serve as vehicles for expressing one's own love of life and devotion to God.

Exploration and experimentation in writing are possible for anyone. The basic resources—pen and paper—are accessible to all, and excellent examples of good writing are found everywhere. Exploring and experimenting with various genres is fun, increases knowledge, and can lead to greater self-understanding, fresh perspective, and personal growth.

The belief that the *story* of our lives matters is a missing piece of the puzzle in American culture. We see around us the brokenness, loneliness and emptiness of at least two generations that have put the individual—the self—first. This is not at all what I mean when I assert that *you matter.*

When the individual self is exalted and the right of individuals to live for themselves is considered the highest priority, the result is disconnection from others, isolation, and a pervasive loss of meaning. Socially this is evidenced in broken homes, violent and non-violent crime, substance abuse, sexual promiscuity and confusion, unwanted pregnancies, and ever-increasing numbers of people in therapy and counseling, to name only a few.

When we speak of the *story* of a person's life, we automatically envision not only the individual, but other people, relationships, family connections. Stories have characters with personalities and stories all their own which weave in and out of each other, forming a rich tapestry. Each person's story gains meaning and significance by its *relationship* to others' stories.

If our lives lack love, it is an inevitability of human nature to look for help, comfort, or some substitute. Consumerism and materialism are as addictive as drugs, and ultimately just as void of real satisfaction even for the affluent. These problems are not confined to one socio-economic stratum of society. We are rich in things, but poor in spirit.

Our inner poverty is evidenced by the paradoxes of a culture that is simultaneously beguiled by the race for ever higher-technology and the pursuit of "things spiritual," movements to recover simpler ways of living coexisting with rampant consumerism, and efforts to rediscover ancestral roots alongside a fascination with a godless future. We are looking for something meaningful, faster all the time!

At bottom, the ability to believe that we matter to someone besides ourselves depends on how we answer the questions of who we are, how we came to be and why we exist at all. The belief that we are created by God, in God's image, for good and meaningful purposes is a belief largely lost in contemporary culture. The loss of this spiritual base contributes powerfully to a culture that has accelerated the flow of information almost beyond imagining, while drastically decreasing the significance of it all. Ted Koppel noted this phenomenon when he received the Broadcaster of the Year award:

> What is largely missing in American life today is a sense of context, of saying or doing anything that is intended or even expected to live beyond the moment . . . Consider this paradox: almost everything that is publicly said these days is recorded. Almost nothing of what is said is worth remembering.[1]

The public media are flooded with endless streams of images and words that are truly not worth remembering, while the stories that are truly meaningful—*personal* stories, valued by those who are the living heroes of those stories— largely go unwritten and therefore, untold. We have collectively abandoned the telling of our own stories to the media in the foolish belief that whatever "professionals" choose to write or tell or show is what really must matter. If you are not on television or in the newspaper, can you really be important? Do you really matter?

This book advocates a revolution that is unlikely ever to make the evening news report because it is a revolution that occurs in the simple, quiet, reflective, self-and-others-affirming act of writing. There is little flash and not much glamour in writing, except for a tiny number of celebrity writers. But in personal writing there is thought, remembrance, creation, emotion, suffering, joy, celebration—all the pleasures and pains that humanize us, make us *persons*, and teach us how inextricably connected we are to one another.

This book, therefore, encourages writing. It is for beginning writers, experienced writers who are pursuing new genres, and "closet writers" who have never shared their writing with anyone else. It is for those who secretly wish to write but have never tried, because they are sure they cannot do it well, and it is perhaps especially for those who simply have never thought of themselves as writers at all.

I hope to inspire you by sharing many benefits of the pleasures of personal writing. The book is full of ideas that will, hopefully, spur you on to try each genre discussed. Its format will accommodate those of you who, like me, *must* write notes in the margins!

The chapters include samples from my own writing and from dear friends who have contributed pieces of their stories. It is, in this regard, unabashedly *personal* writing. My sincere hope is that these selections will encourage you to value your story and inspire those who may be new to the art of writing to make a beginning.

To help you in understanding what I mean by the terms I use, and in exploring the ideas presented here more fully, I have included a glossary and a bibliography. Since my aim is to encourage you to commence, continue, and persevere in writing, consider these provisions for your journey.

The place to start is with this question: Why write?

# Chapter 1

# Foundations:
# God is a Writer

*In the beginning was the Word,*
*and the Word was with God*
*and the Word was God.*
*(John 1:1)*

**W**hy write?

Because God writes.

All life is founded by God and his marvelous creativity. All creative action in a life of faith finds its source in God and his action. All creative action in a life that does not yet know God flows nonetheless from the creative art and soul God has given. The same triune God who said, "Let us make humankind in our image, male and female. . . ," and who created us pure, naked and unashamed in Paradise to enjoy a relationship with him, this same God put the potential for incredible creativity into all people. Writing is the creative action about which we are interested.

*God writes his story.* There is vast evidence in the Bible that God wants the story of his interaction with people to be written down. The prophets were told to write down what they experienced and their messages from God because it mattered to God that his Word and his story be preserved for future generations.

Jesus Christ gives us clues that God takes personal interest in writing about our lives. For instance, after Jesus sent out seventy-two followers, two by two, to announce the kingdom of God, they reported joyously that "even the demons" submitted to them. Jesus himself was full of joy, but warned his followers to rejoice *not* because the spirits submitted to them or were successfully cast out of suffering people, but because "your names are written in heaven" (Luke 10:20).

*Each person who knows Jesus has his or her name "written in heaven in the Lamb's book of life, (Rev. 21:27)."* The names are written there at the instant of conversion, or first prayer of faith, of each newborn child of God. Is your name written there? Do you know for sure that you are named as a child of God? If you are unsure whether your own name is in God's book of life, you have only to ask Jesus Christ to become your savior from sin and the Lord of your life. Allow him to become the Author of your new life in the grace of his complete forgiveness and the blessings of friendship with his people.

If this is not where you are at, perhaps it can be of encouragement to know that God is a seeking God as well as a writing God. He is seeking those he loves, and has given a wonderful promise to all seekers of truth, reality, love and honor, and to all who are seeking a deeper, more honest, reflective life:

> *If you seek the Lord your God, you will find him if you seek him with all your heart and all your soul."*
> *(Deut. 4:29)*

God is "findable" to those seeking the truth about him. Our individual importance to him is affirmed by the fact that God the Father has found us and put us—by name—into his own "baby book." I hope it includes your name, or that it someday will.

Your name is the beginning of your personal history, and all interest in your story begins with interest in your name. Who are you? What are you like? What is your story? Where are you in your life journey? How is God's loving action reflected in your life?

In about 96 A.D., long after the apostle Paul had written his letters by the inspiration of the Holy Spirit, Jesus appeared to his beloved disciple, John, exiled on the Greek island of Patmos, and gave him several visions accompanied by these instructions:

> Write in a scroll what you see . . .          (Rev. 1:11)

> Write what you have seen, and what is now . . .
>                                               (Rev. 1:19)

In context, Jesus was instructing John to write down the visions shown him of what will take place at the end of time. John wrote Jesus' messages to specific churches, as found in chapters 2 and 3. Beginning with Chapter 4, John records a revelation for all churches: the grand drama of the opening of the Book of Life. Those whose names are found in this Book will be invited into the temple of God, into eternal life with him.

Could there ever be a more dramatic reading of a book? The whole universe breathless, waiting to hear whose names are read! This is a book God has been writing since he created the universe, and it is full of names. It is the only book ultimately worth having your name in. It is worth eternal life. When it is read on that day, your name will receive the greatest honor it could ever know, and you the greatest joy.

We can see from these examples that *God is interested in communicating with us and with future generations,* and that his method includes both spoken and written forms of communication. He is also interested in our communicating with others. What strikes me is the simplicity of Jesus' instruction to John in this regard: "Write down what you see."

"To see" carries the idea of perception—what you perceive, what you know and discern, as well as what you observe. Jesus, the living *logos*, or Word, of God, was speaking to John. Yet, I wonder, was he also speaking to us? Does he want everyone to write what we see, what we perceive of life, and of him? Luci Shaw, in her excellent book on journaling, *Life Path*, discusses this at greater length. She feels we can transfer John's commission to our own lives as a call from God to write what we see by journaling. I heartily agree.

*Does God want all his children to write?* No, there is no biblical evidence to suggest that writing is a universal call. God has not made a general command for everyone who loves him to write about his love, but, thank God, he did ask some to do so! Not everyone who loves God has been given a grand vision as John was, or a grand commission as was Paul.

However, God does ask all his children to write his Word "upon the door frames of their houses," (Deut. 6:9) and "on the tablets of their hearts," (Prov. 7:3). Figuratively, God expects every one of his children to be so familiar with his Word that it is within our view every day and written on our hearts, where no one can ever take it away.

Called to write in these ways, we are universally called to tell our children about Him.

> *Hear, O Israel: The LORD our God, the LORD is one. Love the LORD your God with all your heart and with all your soul and with all your strength. These commandments that I give you today are to be upon your hearts. Impress them on your children. Talk about*

*them when you sit at home and when you walk along the*
*road, when you lie down and when you get up.*
                                              *(Deut. 6:4–7)*

If we tell our children about the Lord and his story, we
are not far from the ability to write about his effect on our
lives, our stories. The more we understand his Word and
the more we obey him, the more we will perceive him at
work in our own lives. The more we are empowered to
remember, the more we will have to write.

> A thought merely thought often flies away
> but a thought written down is here to stay.

I made up this ditty sometime in my childhood. It is a
little girl's thought that has colored a woman's world. And
this woman knows herself to be the very same person she
was as a little girl, because she wrote, and she writes.
Congruency—being the same person over time—is a benefit
of long-term personal expression in the written word.

Why do we write? What is our motivation? There are as
many motivations as there are people, I suppose.
Certainly I write because I enjoy writing. I like the process
of seeing the imagination take form. The sense of
capturing on paper thoughts that I don't want to forget is
empowering.

I've been asked if I write because I want to be known. I
used to take that to mean "well-known or famous" and
answered "No!" with some vehemence. "No! I just love
to write," I would say. (Shakespeare would say, "Thou
dost protest too much!") In truth, recognition is part of
the motivation for any form of creativity. Music is made
to be heard, stories are made to be read. Now, if asked
why I write, I answer differently. I love to write, I have
something to say, and I want God to be known through
me—not because I want to be someone famous, but
because I am someone who wants to reflect something of

God's glory. God is the only one who makes any of us into lovely reflections, in some small way, of himself. That we undeserving ones can reflect him at all is such a glory that it deserves to be shared. To become someone known or famous is a benefit, perhaps, but it is not the reason to write.

*The reason to write is that you have something to say—your story!* Many people protest that they have nothing unique to say. "It's all been said before." This is a silly notion! If you are made by God, there is not another person who is *you* on the face of the earth. You have a unique story to share: the story of how you came to be who you are; how you found your marriage partner, if you have one; how you made your friends, and what vocation and avocations you have chosen and why. How you came to know God, how you know him now, and what you are learning from him is also uniquely your story. If what you produce in synthesizing your story and your learning is a familiar idea that has been stated by twenty other people, or two thousand, it is no less unique, for they are not you! Your story carries unique impact even when what you learn is the same thing others learn—about life, about God, or whatever.

Phyllis A. Whitney says in *Guide to Fiction Writing* that writing from your own special knowledge is "the plus factor," that certain something in your writing that publishers look for and readers gobble up. It took her years to discover this, because she wasn't interested in writing about the Orient, where she spent the first fifteen years of her life. It was a powerful discovery for her, when she was already a prolific writer and published author, that her own story mattered so much.

When we start at the foundation of our relationship with Jesus Christ, we have the upper hand on this truth at the inception of our venture with writing, for he is affirming and writing our story with us. We have to learn, though, to value our own story and to see it with new eyes. Write about what is familiar to you—what you know and have experienced firsthand. Just because your story is so familiar to you does not mean it will lack interest for others!

*The more people write about what they have to say, the more they and others have the chance to learn*—to know something new, to see something differently, from a new perspective.

The late D.P. Thompson, a great leader in the Church of Scotland, once associated learning and life in a memorable way for me:

> The moment you stop learning from Everyman
> is the moment you begin to die.

It is desirable to learn from people who have a love of learning. According to Thompson, those who love to learn love life, and that love of life shows itself in the humility to learn from anyone and everyone in some way or other. This means valuing people and their stories, and acknowledging their existence as persons.

I will never forget D.P. Thompson, with bushy white eyebrows shadowing his bright blue eyes, glowering at a group of us young Americans who were in Scotland to learn from him, as he taught us, "When we de-personalize—treat people as objects—we affirm not life, but death. We dehumanize people made in God's image! How can we expect the gas station attendant or whomever we 'object-ify' to know God's love for them? Treat objects as objects and people as persons!"

It follows that the more of us who value our stories enough to write what we are learning, the more others can benefit from our lives. And it follows that the more Christians write about what they have learned, the more we may learn about the Kingdom of God—more or less accurately!

The more we write accurately to the biblical message, the more the Kingdom of God may advance.

Yet even Christian writings that display bad theology (a poor or incomplete understanding of God's character and activity, or poor interpretations of Scripture) have influenced people toward Jesus Christ. I am thinking of much of what sits on the popular Christian bookstore shelves—a lot of "fluff and stuff"—that encourages people to come to faith in Christ but stops short of emphasizing the need to learn, read, question, think critically, and seek maturity in relationship with him. Books that define Christian maturity as conformity to certain legalistic rules, certain ways of voting, certain behaviors, etc., are particularly misleading and a detriment in coming to faith in Christ for those seeking freedom and adventure in life.

There seem to be a lot of "sheep" in American culture who seem to prefer the false, but nevertheless *felt* security and safety of legalisms. Yet they are telling Christ's story to others. The Kingdom of God advances in curious ways!

The fact that there is a lot of "fluff and stuff" on the bookshelves is, in itself, a good reason why we need more people of intellectual integrity to write and more Christian writers to become better informed biblically and theologically.

He may not call all of us to write, but I am sure God would be pleased if more of us would try writing—for our pleasure and for his. For God has gone way beyond the gift of the written Word of the Bible, even beyond the incarnate living Word of his Son. God has given the full measure of himself to us by his Holy Spirit—his indwelling presence from the first moment we ask Christ Jesus to save us from sin and enter into our lives. Having done this, he continues to write himself into our lives, as he promised:

> *I will put my law in their minds and write it on their hearts.*
>
> (Jer. 31:33)

> *I will give you a new heart and put a new spirit in you; I will remove from you your heart of stone and give you a heart of flesh. And I will put my Spirit in you and move you to follow my decrees and be careful to keep my laws.*
>
> (Ezek. 36:26–27)

God's Spirit is the pen with which he writes upon our new hearts.

> *You show [by your lives] that you are a letter from Christ, . . . written not with ink, but with the Spirit of the living God, not on tablets of stone but on tablets of human hearts.*
>
> (2 Cor 3:3)

We are the letters that God is writing to those who seek him. The Writer is the Lord, and the letter is the story of your life and what God has done in it. And the readers are those in your life who are looking for the good news of Christ's love and salvation.

Those who know the Lord show by their lives that God is real, and that his message of love is true and relevant. We are living letters—personal communications through our individual personalities—of God's love and grace. The way some have put it: "You may be the only letter from God someone will ever read!" I've also heard the variation, "You may be the only Bible someone will ever read!" Isn't that a dreadful thought? I'm glad God planned for many of us to be letters from God for all who seek him, and that he preserved, in the Bible, one written set of letters for us all.

But who can read the letter from God that comes through our lives once we are in heaven with the Father? Is there any reason to think that our letters from God, that is, our individual stories, matter once we are gone from this life? I think so. Most people I know, whether they are Christians or not, affect others lives more than they know. Many times, memorial services produce surprises for the family left behind of the great number of people whose lives were touched by the person who died. Often it is many more people than anyone ever could have expected, particularly in relation to Christians who have died.

If we letters from God never write down our stories, then God's touch of love through our lives will be influential only as long as we live. After we die, only for a time will God's love from our stories continue to bless those whose lives we touched most directly.

How many more lives could be touched by God's work in our lives if we wrote it down? Preserving in writing what God did for you, to you and through you will be a blessing to more people than you could imagine. I believe God will see to it, if you write it down.

You matter and your story matters. Your personality matters, because God made you the way you are and lives within you, or is seeking to. Your interests, thoughts, hopes, deep desires, and dreams matter. Your choices matter. The story of God's action in your life—his messages, calls, provisions, comforts and challenges—all this matters, too.

*To whom does your story matter?* To future generations. You are a letter for future generations, if you write out what God has written on your heart.

Your children, grandchildren and great-grandchildren will each likely find, at some time in their lives, that it matters very much to them to know your story.

This curiosity can arise for various reasons. Adopted children often become interested, as adolescents, in knowing more about their birth parents. Adults often realize, as their grandparents or parents pass on, that a great deal of family history held in the memory of the older generations has passed on with them, never to be recovered unless it has been written down or recorded in some fashion. Parents discovering the unique personalities of their young children may want to understand more about the genetic pool from which their children derive! Whatever the motivation for wanting to know more, those who are left a written record of their parents' or grandparents' stories are given a priceless gift, indeed.

Children also look to their parents for faith. Among the endless questions that pre-school-age children ask, it is common to find them asking about God. Many years of ministry with college students has made it clear to me that, even as young adults, children continue to look to their parents for signs as to what to believe, what really matters in life (though they often hide this fact from their parents at that age!).

Scripture states clearly that parents have a special responsibility to tell their children the story of God's faithfulness—but don't think that God wants us only to tell our children Bible stories! What about what *you* can say, because you know the Lord yourself? Your personal story of faith is perhaps the most important story of all for you to tell your children.

> *Tell it to your children, and let your children tell it to their children, and their children to the next generation.*
> *(Joel 1:3)*

*God promises that your obedience to him will positively bless the next generations.* The Bible consistently mentions the impact of our choices to seek (or avoid) God as reaching down with blessing (or curse) to the next generation, even to the next four generations (cf. Numbers 14:18). The power of our story—specifically the story of our faith in God—can have far greater impact than we usually imagine. Your great-great-grandchildren (and even later generations) can be blessed by your life!

> *Know therefore that the LORD your God is God; he is the faithful God, keeping his covenant of love to a thousand generations of those who love him and keep his commands.*
>
> *(Deut. 7:9)*

> *Posterity will serve him; future generations will be told about the Lord. They will proclaim his righteousness to a people yet unborn—for he has done it.*
>
> *(Ps. 22:30, 31)*

We are also instructed to ask our parents and grandparents what they have learned from God. To do so is to give them a wonderful message of how much they matter to us.

> *Ask the former generations and find out what their fathers learned, for we were born only yesterday and know nothing, and our days on earth are but a shadow. Will they not instruct you and tell you? Will they not bring forth words from their understanding?*
>
> *(Job 8:8–10)*

After my grandmother Hazel died, I inherited a beautiful quilt that her mother had made. This reawakened and intensified my interest in that great-grandmother and in why I had been named for her, whom I had never met— too late, sadly, to ask my grandmother. When I read this verse from Job 8, it encouraged me nevertheless to ask my parents for "words from their understanding." I will tell more of that story later.

There are others besides relatives who might benefit from our stories—special friends, for example, and their children. I have a god-daughter named for me. We know a few things about each other. We both know that her parents are special friends of mine, and that we all love Jesus. Yet we barely know each other because we've not lived near enough to see each other very often. I'm quite sure, though, that we would both enjoy knowing more of each other's story.

In spite of all the good reasons we might list for writing, there will always be people who say, "I am not a writer." Are you one who says that you cannot express yourself in the written word, that you are not creative in that way? Perhaps you have judged too quickly. Maybe you have tried to write, but have not had encouragement, guidance, or helpful feedback and have been so frustrated that you just gave up.

Most Americans today decided somewhere between the ages of seven and ten that they were not good at art, according to Mona Brooks in *Drawing with Children*.[1] Similarly, many people decide early in life that writing is too difficult, too time-consuming, or too unrewarding. They have viewed it as work—*school work*—and are glad to be done with it. Many people lack experience with the different forms of creative writing that can be pure pleasure. People who write in the course of their work can feel they are not expressive writers when it comes to the personal dimension of their lives. Others just never had the inclination to write.

However, somewhere in mid-life, just before the children are out of the "nest" or just after they've left home for college or to marry, many parents find the inclination to write. It may be that the ancestral bug has bitten: "Where do I come from? How did God figure into my history?" Or it may be the descendants' bug-bite: "What will my children remember? Will my grandchildren know the hope I held for them, how much I prayed for them? How can I touch the great-grandchildren I may never know with my love?"

A journal entry from my friend Martha reflects exactly the longing we parents have for our children and future generations:

> The Sunday before Suzi called, the choir at the church sang an anthem called Find Us Faithful. The message of the song was powerful! It spoke of our life being a journey; its path lined with faithful folks from the past who are cheering us along. Their lives testify to God's sustaining grace. The following words captured my attention and challenged my heart.

> *But as those who've gone before us,*
> *let us leave to those behind us*
> *the heritage of faithfulness passed on thru godly lives.*
> *O may all who come behind us find us faithful;*
> *May the fire of our devotion light their way.*
> *May the footprints that we leave*
> *lead them to believe*
> *And the lives we live inspire them to obey.*
> *After all our hopes and dreams have come and gone,*
> *And our children sift thru all we've left behind,*
> *May the clues that they discover*
> *And the mem'ries they uncover*
> *Become the light that leads them*
> *to the road we each must find.*
> 

*words and music by Jon Mohr*
*(Hope Publishing Co.)*

> Martha Zimmerman
> Vancouver, 1995

Young mothers may not all have the inclination to write, but they sure have the pressure. The marketplace—from the baby stores to the stationers to the bookstores—displays baby books that send out messages: "You should record your baby's milestones! This is what a caring mother does!" With babies and preschoolers at their knees, many young moms want to write in that cute baby book, but feel they cannot find enough uninterrupted time. Some make the valiant effort with the first child's baby book, yet within a few years, they find they have neglected to keep up with it because another baby or two—and additional books—have come along. Caring non-stop for babies and small children is more than time-consuming—it's emotionally and physically exhausting. Writing happy "first years" memories is an emotional investment that few mothers manage to keep making, over time.

Guilt over unfilled baby books, even when some of those initial "firsts" got recorded, is no motivation for getting started again. Fortunately, there are some young mothers who have found journaling a way to record what they want to remember. Fortunately too, a journal makes no demands to fill in the blanks in a prescribed way. My writing friend, Sarah, is building and leaving a living legacy for her children:

> As a new mother, I start writing in journals to my children (in addition to their baby books) before they are born, to share with them my hopes, fears and dreams for their lives, and to record meaningful events, and milestones that they reach as they grow up.

> Sarah Meekhof
> New York, 1995

You matter, your story matters, and your desire to bless your children and your parents matters—and all these stories matter to God more than to you!

Therefore, *let go of guilt* if you have unfilled baby books. What you decide you can do, rejoice in that. God will see to it that your children develop appropriate self-esteem and happy memories of their childhood even if you didn't get the cutest thing he or she ever said written down. Let go of guilt over diaries and journals that you started and didn't fill.

*Let go of lost knowledge* about your own past and about the past generations whose stories you can no longer recover. God will bless you because of them regardless, and you can make a different contribution to your grandchildren as God leads and empowers you. God's Spirit in us is the one who reminds us of what we need to know—he will help you recover the memories that are important to recover for your writing.

*Let go of fear* as you experiment with creative writing. It is not important to write to some external standard when you are journaling or writing a story, history or poem that expresses something of yourself. It is important not to judge too soon. It is important to say what you mean to say, to look into your heart and reflect and pray. It is important to create what you intend to create.

*Renew your mind about writing.* Let go of self-consciousness. No one is watching you. There is no one else you need to please. When you are venturing in self-expression, it is important to please yourself. This may sound self-centered, but it is profoundly Christian, because no one else can know completely what is in you except you and the Lord. No one but his Spirit within you need be consulted when you are seeking to write about yourself. He will reveal new insights to you and make your self-expression richer, more meaningful and more refreshing to you.

*Finally, it is important to play at writing.* Have fun with it—decide that writing is a form of play for you! "Adults play too," my husband and I tell our children. I cannot abide the idea that play is confined to childhood and responsibility is confined to adulthood. Where did such a grotesque idea come from? In God's world, we all have both!

If you can explore with a spirit set free in Christ's grace to play with writing, and if you find the kind of writing you can enjoy, you will please yourself and your Heavenly Father too. You are his child. He delights to see his children at play, enjoying themselves by imagining, creating, producing creations that are not meant to impress, but to bless. Even if you can only see that your writing blesses you, it is still a blessing and a worthy medium for expressing your story.

You will please God with your writing as you agree with him that indeed you matter, your story matters, and your journey with him matters. Now, as you take a look at journaling, ponder these prayers from the heart of one of the great "journalers" of the Bible, King David:

> *I will perpetuate your memory through all generations; therefore the nations will praise you for ever and ever.*
> *(Ps. 45:17)*

> *I will sing of the Lord's great love forever; with my mouth I will make your faithfulness known through all generations.*
> *(Ps. 89:1)*

# Chapter 2

# Journaling:
# A Journey
# With the Lord

"The horror of the moment," the King went on, "I
shall never, never forget!" "You will though," said
the Queen, "if you don't make a memorandum of it."

Lewis Carroll
*Through the Looking-Glass*

Reflective journaling influences life and faith in
a way that perhaps nothing else can. Though there
are many endeavors which can build and strengthen your
faith, there is nothing quite like the pleasure and deep
satisfaction of keeping a journal of your reflections along
the pathway of your life.

In French, *jour* means day. A journal is a daily account of
life. In this sense it is similar to a diary, a daily record.

I prefer the term *journal* over *diary* for the simple reason
that *journal* carries the concepts of "process" and
"journey." A diarist may keep a record of events but never
go deeper to reflect on the meaning of what has been seen.
Journalers are interested in meaning and learning at a deep
personal level. We are attaching meaning, making
progress, moving in a direction, engaged in a journey—
we are going somewhere.

It has been said of those who write that we love life so
much we live twice—once in our daily lives and again on
paper. That is, we also live in our writing. This certainly
is true for me.

But what about the person who is coming to journal writing for the first time? Inasmuch as everyone has a daily life, everyone has a journey, a story. Thus anyone who can form letters, words and sentences on a page can attempt some form of journaling, some form of record-keeping about his days or her experiences.

Does one have to love writing in order to journal? No. Will everyone who tries journaling come to live in the writing—to find a source of life-nurture in journaling? No, not necessarily. But love of life, or love of humor, love of people, flowers, horses, children—whatever inspires your love—is something worthwhile for you to write about as part of your journey through life. In writing about what you love, you will begin to live in the writing as you find ways to express your own thoughts and feelings and attach your own meanings to what you record. As the love that motivates you to write gives itself back to you, you will find refreshment and pleasure in journaling.

For any person, journaling is a way of tracking one's own walk through life. There is an objectifying process of reflection that happens when we write down our walk through the day or the week or the year and let it sift through our minds and hearts. It is a form of living twice—or re-experiencing—to record one's journey and then, through introspection, to reflect upon its impact. In writing one's response to the meaning of a particular experience, one again lives that part of the journey on a richer and deeper level of understanding.

For the person of faith in Christ, the journey is a walk through life in companionship with one's self and the Spirit of God within. The reflective process becomes sanctified introspection, looking at the self and one's life with the vision of one's eyes and heart filtered by Christ's love, truth and grace. Progress is growth along the way: maturation, insight, healing, comfort, challenge, enrichment, empowerment. The journey is toward wholeness and purity before God—fitness for heaven—and the destination is eternal enjoyment of God and all that is his.

Keeping track of my journey as Christ's person puts me in touch with the intersection of spiritual and earthy reality, of the "already and not yet" nature of our existence as God's people. Those who know Jesus Christ are already living eternally. It is so from the inception of our faith in Christ, as Scripture declares. Yet we are living in bodies that must suffer decay and death. The inherent tension of this paradox creates the opportunity for any believer to benefit from journaling about the struggles of living in this dual reality. God's indwelling Spirit can create the motivation for anyone to practice some form of journaling, and make it a pleasure.

The way journaling puts me in touch with life is somewhat of a mystery to me because I sense God in an intensely personal way when I address questions and issues of my life on paper before him. He has shown me things, prompted critical questions, uncovered things, freed and healed me in ways I could never have expected were I not writing down what was really inside me.

I can best describe the fundamentals of journaling by telling you what I use, what I do, how and why I do it, and show you by examples some of the many benefits of journaling.

### Approach and choice of means
I hold one presupposition about the best approach to reflective journaling: a journal should be written by hand. Do not, as a matter of daily life, keep your personal journal on a computer. I am not against progressive technology, but the artful experience of connecting with yourself and with God at a deep level is more personal and sensed more easily when you actually take the time to reflect, at ease and relaxed. In relaxation one can experience the "flow" of heart connecting with mind and

hand. With a computer, you almost have to be at a desk. With a bound empty book, you can be anywhere you like, anywhere you are comfortable.

Your own hand-written words are part of you and, if like mine, may be more difficult to read than a typed script. This can be an advantage if you lose your journal! As long as your name, address and phone number inside the front cover are legible, that is all that must be understandable to anyone else.

Beyond this there is not one "right way" to approach journal keeping. You are free to journal any way you like. Your choice of books, however, will make some difference in your experience of the process. Some journals will seem more utilitarian, thus possibly less inviting, yet I personally like the utilitarian spiral notebooks with college ruled paper and no dividers. They are helpful, easily accessible, and convenient (purse or pocket-size).

My favorite journal is the kind with heavy cardboard covers, no lines, thick paper so the ink from my fountain pen doesn't leak through, and wire rings that bind the pages. They open flat—you needn't hold them open— and they go anywhere. For many years I journaled at night in bed. I preferred a large (8 1/2 by 11) spiral notebook with thick cardboard cover for that time and place. It is useful for poetry; you can fit a decent-sized poem, with corrections, on one page. A large journal also provides more space to rest your hand while you are musing and the pen is still.

You may enjoy the pretty bound journals that you can find in bookstores and gift shops. These usually have ruled, numberless pages and a sturdy binding, plus, they look lovely on your desk or bookshelf. If aesthetics are important to you, you may prefer these even though they are more pricey. I enjoy taking a pretty bound journal with me to worship, one that stacks neatly with my Bible if it doesn't fit in my purse, for taking notes.

*How many journals do you need?* Over the last thirty years, my approach to journaling has evolved from keeping one diary to keeping three or four journals at a time and then back to keeping one.

During one lengthy period, I had one journal for spiritual growth, another for travels and vacations, and a third for poetry and daily loggings and reflections. Actually, reflections were recorded and questions arose in all three books. If my spiritual journal was left at home on a trip, I always missed it, for it tended to be more reflective than either of the other two, which were more descriptive and subjective. It was impossible to keep content neatly segregated like we tried to keep our lives in those days of the 70's, when we talked about "my Christian life" in contrast with "the rest of my life!" My spiritual journal had to be with me in every place where preaching, teaching or spiritual wisdom might pop up. Eventually, I realized I needed to keep it with me everywhere I went! God turned my serious intent to learn of him into a delightful adventure. Looking for God everywhere, you find him at the most unsuspected moments and with the most unlikely people.

Particularly during my "baby making" years, when baby book journaling became important, I had to move to only one journal of my own. It was hard enough to keep one with an additional baby book for each child who came along.

Over the last dozen years, the growth, work, travels, special events and reflections, the poetry—everything I like to write about or record or create—has landed in one book, one journey-keeping journal. Using one journal now seems more integrated with actual experience. *The benefit of keeping one journal for everything is seeing one's life as a whole*—the way we live it day by day.

How many different kinds of journals you keep at one time will depend on how many uses you have in mind, and how you want to be organized.

### Organizing your journal

Organization of your journal is important if you want to reread and reflect over your recorded experiences. I have not yet graduated to the discipline of numbering pages and categorizing certain thoughts at the back of the book that I will want to find again, as other experienced journalers advise.

You may find this helpful. It means disciplining yourself to reread your journal at some point in order to do the numbering and categorizing, unless you take the time to do it as you go. I find these approaches too tedious. When I reread my journals, as long as the entries are dated and the city or event noted at the top of the page, I can find what I want. It is far easier to lock in on memories searching one book with labels in the same place on each page than sorting through three!

You may find that a date and brief description of your journal entry is helpful at the top of each page—journal entry, notes from a poetry lecture, quote from a favorite professor, memory, Bible study on John 3:1-15, my child's latest escapade. When you want to find something you recorded at an earlier time, you will be glad to have these reference points.

You will want to find out for yourself what kind of journals, and how many at a time, you will use and enjoy most. There are journals for just about every conceivable purpose: gardening, Grandmother's memories, traveling and holidays, plus many more. You will find a great variety of options, including ones with "built in" drawings, significant thoughts, or Bible verses. Explore and see what fits.

### Define your purpose for journaling

The purpose you choose for your journal will be the greatest influence on your experience of writing about your journey. My purposes have varied over time as described above. Any purpose you choose that is important to you will be rewarding.

One purpose for my journal is note-taking. Writing down the significant things I hear always gives my mind something to chew on, return to, and it helps me remember more accurately. When I've needed to lead a Bible study or teach a Bible lesson, it has been convenient to have biblically-sound sermon notes to refer to in my journals. Note-taking precedes learning, accompanies reflecting, and assists remembering. Having notes to refer to affords the opportunity to expand knowledge, and to share it.

In an age smothered with words that often mean nothing to us (junk mail, billboards, tabloids, etc.), it is rewarding to capture words that are worth remembering. Students and writers, poets and playwrights take notes. So do leaders. Many people in management take notes on every conversation, use tape recorders, and employ staff to help them secure in writing what must be documented. But for the rest of us, is note-taking becoming a lost art? I pondered the question in my journal:

> So few people take notes of any kind, so few Christians take sermon notes. Have I become complacent? I never hear me encouraging anyone, except children through college age—the changeable ones!—to take *any* kind of notes anymore. I must be intimidated.
>
> Would note-taking benefit others as it does me? Or am I just dull-minded and *must* have visualization

to complete my memory!? Maybe others *do* remember what is most important to them without extra effort. Anyway, it is not extra effort for me. I cannot help wondering though, what lies deeper? Do we Christians unconsciously feel we already know anything we might hear on a Sunday morning? Do we secretly think God has nothing new or fresh to say to us? We would never say so. Maybe most Christians are auditory learners? (I seriously doubt this, but we *act* like it!) Anyway, *I'm* not exclusively auditory—happily! Visualizing words and drawing concepts takes me deeper in understanding and helps me remember . . .

Susan Paul
Richland, 1995

Just about any purpose you choose for your journal writing can be beneficial to personal or spiritual growth without that being your specific aim. For instance, suppose you decide to journal about your gardening endeavors. As the Great Gardener works in you, you may be amazed at how many "garden" scriptures come to mind and come alive to you. As you deepen your love for and broaden your understanding of gardening you will find that writing about what you learn will reveal parallels in other parts of your life.

The Great Gardener sowed many new seeds in my heart when I entrusted my life to him at age 19. One seed was a new love for working with junior high youth that grew through my friendship with Merrie Goddard when she was 13. Merrie became a dear friend then and continues to be today, many years later. One of the many purposes she finds for her journal is a place to respond to Scripture as she reflects upon it.

*Jesus told them another parable: "The kingdom of heaven is like a man who sowed good seed in his field.*

*But while everyone was sleeping, his enemy came and sowed weeds among the wheat, and went away. When the wheat sprouted and formed heads, then the weeds also appeared. The owner's servants came to him and said, 'Sir, didn't you sow good seed in your field? Where then did the weeds come from?' 'An enemy did this,' he replied. The servants asked him, 'Do you want us to go and pull them up?' 'No,' he answered, 'because while you are pulling the weeds, you may root up the wheat with them. Let both grow together until the harvest. At that time I will tell the harvesters: First collect the weeds and tie them in bundles to be burned; then gather the wheat and bring it into my barn.'"*

*(Matt. 13:24-30)*

O Lord, there are weeds in me that you refuse to take up. And there are weeds in other people— that I will live with, lest I pull up their roots. . . . O please, by your infinite mercy—allow me to bear fruit—because, O Lord, I love you.

Merrie Goddard
Strasbourg, 1995

Merrie is a prolific reader and a gifted writer. In France one summer we participated in a study seminar together. After we read Pascal's *Pensées* (French for "thoughts") and studied Martin Luther's *Freedom of the Christian Man* in combination with the book of Galatians, we all wrote our own *pensées:*

*For freedom Christ has set us free; stand fast therefore and do not submit again to a yoke of slavery.*

*(Gal. 5:1)*

A Christian is a perfectly free lord of all, subject to none. A Christian is a perfectly dutiful servant of all, subject to all.

Martin Luther

Living in this tension of Christian servant-leadership is the practical definition of "walking in the Spirit." Grace requires of us a longing for freedom. We so often prefer our own lament to a freedom out of our control. When we dare to relinquish our power and receive Christ's forgiveness, Grace overwhelms us with terror and delight! Freedom requires of us a longing for Grace.

Merrie Goddard

Define the purpose for your journal with sensitivity to what your life situation is at this time. If times are stressful, you may need your journal to be the private place where you can release tension and find relief. If times are fairly on balance, you may wish to use your journal to explore some questions you left waiting unanswered for a better time. Or you may wish to take advantage of the relative happiness of the time to record what you are grateful for—the joys and pleasures of life as you see them.

I find that recording my prayers and God's answers and writing out my thanksgiving to him actually holds me to the discipline of gratitude. Those who know Jesus Christ as the Lord have so much to be grateful for, so much hope. Some of us need to find ways to help ourselves take the time to express that gratitude. Journaling is one way.

My friend and prayer partner, Julie, tells the story of when and why she started journaling:

Journaling began for me when I learned I was pregnant with my older son in 1986. My husband Roy encouraged me to write down my feelings and experiences as a legacy for our son. I've since filled several books with my writings, some of a strictly record-keeping nature; some, my true feelings about a situation; and some, depending on the time of life, cries from my heart.

My journals are invaluable to me. When I read back through them I discover areas of growth, find reassurance that my instincts about something were right in retrospect, and I gain even more confidence that God's hand has been firmly on me in even the worst times. The instances of answers to prayer are overwhelming!

I also see where I need to continue to grow—the journal is a firm reminder that I make some mistakes over and over, and I'm convicted and encouraged (or sometimes shamed) into trying again. Most of all, my journals are a non-threatening, unique, wholly personal reminder of who I've been, who I am and who I want to be.

Julie Gephart
Richland, 1995

Experiencing God's presence is one reason I love to journal. You can be sure that whatever your purpose, if you acknowledge the Lord in the process of journaling, he will make his presence known somehow. I find his presence in the new questions and understandings that come during journaling. He takes great pleasure in our seeking after him for wisdom and understanding. He promises that we shall find wisdom if we seek it as hidden treasure, (cf. Proverbs 2:1-11).

Seeking wisdom and understanding broadens the journaling experience and guards it from becoming overly sentimental and subjective. I have found it helpful to keep my Bible at hand when journaling. There are many times when a question pops into my head and takes me into God's Word. Vice-versa, when I am studying the Bible, I keep my journal at hand, for this is where I write down the new insights I want to remember.

The truthful nature of God's Word cleanses, clarifies and cuts to the core of things that are important. The Bible reflects reality. The full range of earthy human emotion and behavior is captured in Scripture, inviting us to own the full range of our emotions honestly before God, as David did in the Psalms. I am an emotionally honest and forthright person, but I desire not to reflect in my behavior the full range or intensity of my emotion as much as I sometimes do. Writing out my feelings allows for honest expression without undue self-criticism or self-absorption.

In *Cry of the Soul*, an excellent treatise on the Psalms by Dan Allender and Tremper Longman, self-absorption is described:

> Self-absorbed preoccupation with our inner world runs contrary to spiritual maturity. Excessive introspection can lead to a false sense of independence [from God] by giving us the illusion that we can exert control over our lives and become masters of our fate. This path leads too easily to arrogance or confusion.
>
> [We encourage] . . . honest inward examination for the purpose of gaining wisdom—not only to explore the question "what's going on here?" but even more, to respond to what we discover as we ask "what am I doing with God?"[1]

Though they are not addressing journaling *per se*, I agree with Allender and Longman. Journaling with a heart open to God's Spirit helps us maintain the healthy balance that keeps introspection objectified and directed toward God. There can be merely a pale experience of God's loving presence, or little hope for gaining his wisdom, if introspection becomes excessively self-focused and self-directed rather than Spirit-led.

My friend Cindy is a reflective person who seeks this healthy balance. She describes an aspect of this balance in one of her *pensées*:

> In seeking God's will, we would do well to ask not where it is that He wants us but what it is that He wants to do in us where we are.

> Cindy Bennett
> France, 1995

At the end of a summer studying in France, she wrote:

> Have You Noticed?  God Changed.
> . . . try shattering a concrete pillar which has been only reinforced over the years, and you'll find it's a lot of work.  And, when you shatter several of those pillars at once, you also find that the roof falls down all around you.  At least this was my experience this summer.

> I have come to see that it was a good thing God tore  those idols down, that He shattered His old image, that He changed.  It has caused me to make a choice:  either to sit amidst the rubble of wrong religious ruin, or to rebuild according to redeemed reality.

> I am rebuilding.

> Cindy Bennett
> Massachusetts, 1995

For 15 years of her life, Cindy saw God as a grand employer who asked her to abandon who she was to do his work.  He was the distant standard-keeper, watching her struggle to achieve perfection.

Cindy's story illustrates that, for some of us, our journey in childhood in relation to God may have caused us to see him inaccurately. Wrong perceptions of who God is can cause us to feel removed from him—not because he is distant, but because we have not drawn near to him as he really is.

God's presence may also be difficult to experience during times of overwhelming loss and pain. This does not mean God is not there. In excruciatingly painful times, such as after the death of a loved one, I have not been able to sense God's presence with me. I believed he was there, but I could not feel him when I was alone, not even when journaling. Such times call for an extra measure of trust.

A person dealing with unrelenting grief or depression seldom senses God's presence. Such a person may rationally know and believe God is there, and yet be experientially disabled for a time. In my case, this was true only when I was alone. I could feel his presence within me when I was with other people, especially on Sunday mornings in the sanctuary. This was a saving grace that helped me weather a difficult time.

I am accustomed to dealing with pain through journal-keeping, yet my journaling falls apart when God seems not to be there. When God seems to be absent, the prospect of looking deeply into oneself can be horrifying. For a time, I did not want to journey into a place filled with all the darkest emotions, unfathomable pain, "unanswerable" questions and grief without sensing his Spirit's presence. After my brother's death, my journal was closed for a two-month period . In that time, God gave me other gifts in writing, other ways to express myself, that brought me through. Eventually strengthened, I was able to return to my journal and begin to deal with some of the pain. Journaling through pain is excruciating, even in the strength of the Lord.

It can be confusing and hurtful for long-time journalers to not find God when they have come to their journals counting on his merciful presence. I learned though, that we cannot presume to demand as a right what we are accustomed to receiving from God as a gift. The *experience* of his presence is a gift of his Spirit. We have his Spirit's presence at all times, but we cannot expect to constantly experience the *feeling* of his presence when, in our pain or at our own convenience, we demand it.

I have not found other writers who discuss times when journaling may not work for them. Maybe it always works for others, according to their purpose. Certainly not everyone who journals desires to experience God while journal-keeping.

However, since journaling has not always worked for me, perhaps because I do wish to experience God while reflecting and journaling, it is important to tell you what I have learned. If you become incapable of maintaining a spiritual discipline in journaling or in anything else which you normally love and enjoy, and when you hurt over this loss, God will provide another way.

God will give you another outlet if you need to write but cannot seem to do so in your normal pattern. At those worst of times in my life, God blessed me with the mercies of poetry, prose and stories as writing outlets. These gave pleasure, amusement and joy in the midst of grief.

God is good to his children. He absolutely does not leave us during times of devastation. But he probably will surprise us in where and how he meets us, in order to keep us looking for and finding him. He will provide us new outlets for our pain and for our dear desire to affirm life in the midst of tragedy, death and suffering.

### The Many Uses and Benefits of Journaling

Most of the time, people in the midst of crises find solace and strength in journaling. For many people, deep pain and overwhelming loss become the occasion for opening a journal for the first time, to sort things through on paper, to learn, to stay sane, or to stay close to God. Journaling works. The reflective process brings comfort, perspective, endurance and healing to people who journal even though they may not seek God in the midst of their painful process. You can find many books by people who began the process of overcoming crises by journaling.

Luci Shaw, an author and poet, came to journaling when her first husband was diagnosed with cancer. She credits journaling with keeping her so aware of God's action in meeting her needs that she was spared from coming to the brink of emotional breakdown following her husband's death.

> When I am feeling emotional pain, pain that is almost unbearable, I have learned to express it in words on my journal page. Once I write out the pain it seems to draw the sting out of it and make it bearable. *There is the pain on the page.*[2]

What Luci describes—the pain on the page—is true to my own experience. There is a release of the heaviness that accompanies pain, once it is expressed on the page of the journal. I picture Jesus taking it onto himself as I release it to him on the page. He bears its heavy weight.

The most freeing quality of a journal's empty page is its complete lack of judgment. It will take anything you put down, the same way that God takes anything you say to him, whether gratitude, hurt or anger. The shelter of his safety is one good reason I journal.

God is completely non-judgmental about our feelings, though perfectly aware when our feelings are off-center or unjustified. God made us with feelings and, thankfully, he made them to change. He values your feelings, no matter what they are. Yet, he is not moved by them to judge you for them, or necessarily to approve you for them. Rather, God is there to help you journey through whatever you feel, to bring perspective and to help change those feelings which are inappropriate or unhelpful. He will guide you to know what, if any, action is needed.

Because of this sheltering freedom to express the gamut of our feelings, journaling connects us with the Holy Spirit who produces self-control in our lives. Journaling has been a great help to me in this area, for self-control by the Spirit is a very different experience than self-control by the self through repression, denial or self-inflicted guilt. Self-control by the Spirit liberates me from self-destructive choices. His control yields strength, refreshment, relaxation, and freedom to enjoy the benefits and laugh at the problems of being human, while experiencing profound assurance that God's forgiveness covers all our sin.

Another benefit of reflective journaling is inner peace and contentment. Memories are stirred, great moments of joy are relived, the heart is warmed by what one truly values—for me, family, friends and the Lord himself. Through reflection the mind is enabled to think deeply, to probe the heart, and to come to new points of decision that are essential to growth and maturity.

Some have called this process "gaining control of your own life." I suppose that is a fair assessment, for reflection enables us to discern what is and what is not within our own discretion. However, I find the description of journaling as "gaining control" at odds with the reality that much of the stuff of life is *not* within our control. I use the process of writing out my thoughts, questions, and doubts to give control of my life over to God. I seek his help to sort it all out, show me what to do with it, what to decide, and what to hope.

*I will stand at my watch and station myself on the rampart; I will look to see what he will say to me... For the revelation awaits an appointed time; it speaks of the end and will not prove false. Though it lingers, wait for it; it will certainly come and will not delay.*

*(Habakkuk 2:1 & 3)*

Last Sunday in Monterey was a special time. My dear friend, Norma, and I shared this passage from Oswald Chamber's *My Utmost for His Highest*, May 2. It was just what I needed to hang onto. I'm taking it as a word from you, Lord — at last! Thank you, God!

Debbie Fletcher
Monterey, 1994

My dear friend, Debbie, found hope in a devotional study; a word from the Lord to hang onto during a difficult time. This is a wonderful way to use one's journal, to track an answer to our prayer and write a love letter to the Lord.

Other times, a journal is the place to write out our observations, what we see and hear. Here are the words of two friends, the first on a short-term mission, and the second serving as a missionary long-term:

The power was out last night, but we managed with a few candles. A crowd of 150 men were gathered on the ground in front of Ian & Caralee's apartment, in the pitch blackness, watching a small black and white television that was sitting on the hood of a car, powered by the car battery. The occasion: World Cup Soccer, and from the sound of cheering, Brazil was winning. I was so tired, wondering if I would be able to sleep with the resounding echo of excitement, voices bouncing off one apartment building and another. But, what great fun they were having! In spite of the desolation of their lives, for this one hour, nothing else mattered. —Lord, bring men and women who can reach into their dark world with the Truth of who you are and lasting joy!— I don't recall falling asleep. My ear plugs were on the table next to me in the morning.

Margie Gilchrist
Korçë, Albania, 1994


We have electricity tonite. It seems almost anti-climactic . . . so simple. Yesterday we had none . . . today we have. Like C.S. Lewis's conversion. Such a revolutionary and amazing change in our lives should bring fireworks and marching bands (roll of drums and crash of cymbals). The fact that we are now plugged in serves up a good many implications for potential changes in everyday life. Now we can listen to tapes <u>any</u>time. I can make mayonnaise day or nite, as well as iron, sew or listen to the radio. The Sand Man may not always call at 11 p.m.—we can now be nite owls. It is called progress . . . from primitive to pioneer to civilization. The lites seem twice as brite as they were when empowered by the generator. It's as if they've been given a double dose of vitamins. The kids were amazed to see something happen when the lite switch was pushed before 7 p.m. Gone are the compulsory candle-lite dinners—now they will only come by choice. Bedtime will also be a choice. And while the lites pose no limitation now, my body still does . . . and it is yawning and longing for bed. Nite all.

Judy Palpant
Kenya, 1981

Because of the many benefits of journaling, those of us who have tasted its fruits miss it intensely when we have gone starving for reflection. Listen to my eloquent friend describe a "breather of reflection" after a dry spell.

It has been a long time since I have done any serious journaling, and this, I am afraid, will lack the effort of that discipline. I have, however, found myself at loose ends: alone on the SPU campus for a couple of hours. This time is a gift from God to collect my thoughts, perhaps think some new ones, and to simply be quiet and enjoy my coffee for a while.

While on campus, the past briefly emerged today. I saw Mark Purcell from Paris-Alongside days. He said that his last memory of me was of me and Alex Paul dancing at the Frossard's wedding. It makes me wonder how he saw me those three years ago when I was definitely not at my best. So much has happened. So much change. Yet, I am recognizable. I wonder what is different about me. Am I more sure than that gawky young woman who was still trying to find out who she was? Did I appear different to someone who knew me briefly in that far-off time and place? Suzi called me elegant! Am I? I see other women who are gracious and elegant and I wonder: could I be like them? Inconceivable!

I suppose in much of this I must decide what I am going to be. How I view myself affects the view others take of me. Does my confusion about whether I am a kid or an adult communicate itself to other people? I think so. Being an adult does not mean that I have no more questions, no more insecurities. I know this. And yet I create a higher standard for myself than I do for anyone else. Perhaps it's in how I handle those fears and questions that is the difference between kid and adult. Deciding I'm going to act like one may be half the battle. There is no magic here, only reality. Only reality. And that's better than smoke and mirrors.

I am a traveler on a road—I do not know if it is long or short—caught up in something far greater than I can imagine, because of Jesus. If I am conscious of this movement forward, I should be conscious as well of the learning that has taken place as I have walked. I am not the same . . . My teacher is Love itself . . . I am changed . . . It is the journey and its redemption through Jesus that is unique. I am unique and dearly loved. Lord, grant that I see this and my failures in light of the reality of the Kingdom.

I have done little reflecting these last months. I was functioning, but not really living. Reflection is so much a part of my nature; I was living under deprivation. God has allowed me to [come to] West Side. I have been granted some newness. What will I do with it? Shall I continue in fear and persistent questions under a childish system or will I live a devotional life? I must decide this . . . Lord, fill me again with a deep love for you, and for life. It cannot be carefully rationed, only enjoyed as it comes.

Manya White<br>Seattle, 1994

People who make excellent servant-leaders and wonderful disciplers of others in the church are often people who have contemplative natures. It is a temptation to every contemplative to become less involved in the discipline of reflection during times of intense service, when we need the empowerment and peace it provides the most. Manya was embarking on a venture of intense service for several

months in our church at this point in her journey. She felt
she was still a bit too much a kid for the adult shoes she
was putting on. She discovered that the shoes fit her well.
I am so glad she received that "breather" from the Spirit
to take stock of where she was and see her options.

God gives those whose natures are contemplative these
"breathers of reflection" at important junctures in our
journeys, even if we have been less disciplined in reflection
than we wished. God knows our needs, and he will see
that they are met when we are walking in obedience to his
call on our lives.

Journaling for the purpose of synthesizing a specific
significant experience is beneficial even when regular
journaling is impossible for a season. We cannot always
keep a daily or regular journal when demanding
circumstances overwhelm and consume all our energies for
weeks, months, and even years at a stretch. Once we get
some relief, see some progress, find some hope and get
some rest from such rigorous experiences, writing and
reflecting about what we have been through often produces
a clear analysis of what God has been teaching us about
himself.

Such is the case with our friends Greg and Kathleen Moore,
who, with hearts full of love, adopted a beautiful 3 1/2-
year-old boy from Bulgaria, an orphan. Gregory, they
discovered, had never bonded with anyone and was full of
anger, fear, and grief. He responded to their love with
violent rebuffs to "protect" himself from attachment. Here
is a synthesis of their experience and learning:

> Gregory was determined not to love us, trust us,
> need us or want us. He preferred superficial
> relationships which allowed him to remain in
> control . . . and feel "safe."

We began "attachment therapy" with Gregory. We wrapped him in a blanket and held him for hours at a time, forcing eye contact while he raged and thrashed. We didn't allow him to interact with other adults, teaching him to invest in a relationship with us, his parents, in order to have his needs for comfort and attention met. We forgave him daily for the hurts, physical and emotional, that he caused us, and continued to "woo" him even when he was unlovable.

We soon saw parallels between the kind of relationship we were striving for with Gregory and the kind of relationship our Heavenly Father wants to have with us. He woos us when we are unlovable, and adopts us at great cost to Himself. He forgives us continually. More than anything else, His desire is to have a "face to face" relationship with us. He longs for us to run to him first to have our needs met. He wants us to love Him and trust Him enough to yield control of our lives to Him. Sometimes I think He even wraps us in a blanket and lets us thrash around until we relax, cuddle up and gaze into His face.

Many of us have been wounded by life and others, just as little Gregory has. We are so full of anger, fear and grief that we hold God at arms' length, afraid to allow Him control over our lives, afraid to look into His eyes. However, just as infants are born needing a close relationship with their parents, we are created to be in close, intimate relationship with our Creator. He is there, wooing, loving, forgiving, ready to hold us close.

Kathleen Moore<br>
Auburn, 1995

The Moores' long journey with Gregory has come a long way; there is much progress, much to celebrate. I celebrate Greg and Kathleen, Kyla, Haley and Gregory for their faithfulness under God's faithfulness. Their story reflects so clearly that love is a choice—a daily, determined choice.

A journal is an available friend, not a demanding one. It will be there and will not complain if you leave it unattended. In whatever way you approach it, with whatever purpose, no matter how long you are out of touch with the process it affords you, you will find a ready friendship and an adventure of discovery when you take it up again.

### Getting Started
There are many ways to make a start if you have not journaled before, or for a long time. Take the thought off the top of your head—where does it lead you? What is the niggling worry at the back of your mind or that paper-cut slice on your heart? Explore it. What is the hope that drives you? What energizes you and what absolutely wears you out?

There are many books to inform you and plenty of enthusiastic journalers to talk to who will give you well-intended start-up questions to answer, such as, What color best describes you today? (scarlet? mauve? puce?) or, What is the situation of your life at this time? (asleep? awake? surviving?)

Don't misunderstand me, I love questions and revel in them. Many of these used and reused starter questions can be helpful. And there are usually some in every book, luckily, that will hit just the right spot where a novice can make a start.

Answering questions, even silly ones, is part of the fun and playfulness of journaling—no one said it should all be serious! You have freedom to be carefree, whimsical, and nonsensical in your journal. Sometimes other peoples' "off the wall" ideas will give you this freedom.

I've often felt that other's start-up questions were tangential to where I was in a given moment. Yet, I can enjoy following tangents. In doing so, I have found that even those of us who do not need other's starter questions in order to journal can find some fascinating associations and discoveries that we might not otherwise have found without following their silly or tangential question.

Thus, while I can enjoy and am sometimes inspired by others' suggested start-up questions, I usually prefer my own. The questions that arise from inside are nearly always closer to the heart of where I am, and I enjoy playing with them as they arise from my imagination.

Usually when I reflect, questions arise in my mind. My journal is open and I write them down. Sometimes there are no questions, sometimes there are more questions than I have the energy to pursue. Thus I find it helps to ask Jesus to give me the questions I need to pursue:

> Lord, how shall I begin?  Give me Your idea.
> Will you walk and play with me today?
> Connect me to your Spirit and write on my heart today.
> Fill my mind with the questions You have for me.

One of the best discoveries I've made is that asking the Lord to give me the questions—the questions he wants me to deal with—works! For me, this is a wonderful short-cut straight to him. It is also a short-cut to getting focused on what is important when I don't have time for tangents.

Unexpected self-understanding often comes from the questions Jesus gives us. One night, while visiting a friend back East, I suddenly found myself oddly curious why a nearly forty-year-old woman—me—was closing the closet door before hopping into bed.  I was not sleepy yet, so I sat in bed with my open journal looking at those pretty, white-slatted closet doors. "Is that a question you want me to pursue tonight, Lord?"  I chuckled, thinking how silly I am.  Instantly, I felt as if the Lord were saying, "Yes! Why not?  Have fun with it."

I wrote out the question and looked at it for a second or two, pondering.  A few funny memories popped into my head. I wrote them down and chuckled again remembering myself as a child: turning off the hall light and scampering into bed only after looking behind the bedroom door; making a running leap for the bed and then hanging my head over the side of the mattress to check underneath— for snakes—before my brother turned the bedroom light off and walked nonchalantly to his bed.  Suddenly, I *was* a child again, remembering many nights when I had awakened screaming from nightmares, thinking that King Kong—that huge, scary gorilla—had somehow shrunk himself down and was crouching in my closet, ready to spring out, expand and eat me up.

Yes, that was where the habit of closing the closet door had begun.  When I was little, Mother used to check the closet for me to be sure that nothing was there, and then close it for me.  Later, I adopted the same routine for myself.  Some thirty years later, in a new environment, I had fallen back on the same old childhood habit and found that the habit had outlived the fear.  Or had it . . . ?

The next question led me to a deeper fear that was residing in a closet in my heart that night.  What started out as a silly act and a whimsical curiosity led to a pleasant exploration of childhood bedtime fears, and from there to a serious fear (which probably evoked the old habit of closing the closet door at bedtime—something I usually do not do anymore). My fear that night was actually bigger than King Kong, but by writing it out and seeing it for what it was, I was able to return to faith and enjoy a deep sleep.

What memories from your childhood will come to mind as you journal? What discoveries will you make about yourself and how you have matured and changed? What questions will pop into your mind as you pursue your heart? I cannot promise that you will always like yourself better for what you find, but I can assure you that in journaling you will find benefits. Whether you need to focus on what is happening in your story now or to reform your perceptions of the past, whether you need laughter or a place to write out the pain, the pages of your journal will unconditionally welcome your story, because you matter.

# Chapter 3

# Poetry and Prose: A Garden of Graces

Had I the heavens' embroidered clothes
Enwrought with golden and silver light
The blue and the dim and the dark clothes
of Night and light and the half-light,
I would spread the clothes under your feet.
But I, being poor, have only my dreams;
I have spread my dreams under your feet;
Tread softly, because you tread on my dreams.[1]

W. B. Yeats

Poetry and prose are what dreams are made of. Poetry is the lilt and joy, the smile and praise, the art of words and meanings woven together beautifully into a tapestry of love, of celebration, of risking the heights and plummeting the depths of human experience and all we wish to understand. Poetry is a ballad without the music that yet makes music in our souls when we take the time to read it. Poetry sings and causes the reader and writer to do the same.

Poetry plumbs the depths of despair, of darkness and deceit, of love lost or never found, of death and all that accompanies it. Poetry exalts the ordinary, puts the humor into the dull, dismantles pride and lifts what is humble. Poetry weeps, and moves the writer and the reader to do the same.

Poetry is not only undaunted by that which cannot be understood; poetry exults in the mystery of life. G.K. Chesterton puts it this way:

> Poetry is sane because it floats easily in an infinite sea; reason seeks to cross the infinite sea, and so to make it finite. The result is mental exhaustion. To accept everything is an exercise, to understand everything a strain. The poet desires . . . a world to stretch himself in. The poet asks only to get his head into the heavens. It is the logician who seeks to get the heavens into his head. And it is his head which splits.[2]

Poetry is a gift of words in verse, rhyme and meter that waters our hearts with the "yes" of all that we experience. Poetry is multi-sensory in its impact and therefore carries with it a power similar to that of music and drama. Poetry embraces life. Poetry enriches life. Poetry pictures life, and "tells it slant," in the words of Emily Dickinson:

> Tell all the truth, but tell it slant. Truth must dazzle gradually, else all who see be blind . . .[3]

Prose is what you have just read. Prose is actually anything you write or say in a commonplace way. Something that is straightforward and plain (better), or dull and lacking in imagination (worse) may be called "prosaic." You will find prose on every book shelf and in every conversation. It is the common currency of verbal communication.

Prose is an umbrella term used to describe all written and spoken verbiage that is not verse. Prose can tell it straightforwardly, like you read it in the newspaper, or it can tell it slant.

Jesus' prose—especially the stories he told known as parables—often told it slant. He did not explain them all because the stories themselves invite discovery. Grounded in nature and daily life, even two thousand years later his metaphors-in-prose still carry the force to grace our lives with love and truth, to dazzle us gradually with his sovereignty and servant heart.

Poetry speaks of the same stuff of life you could describe in prose, but differs in technique. Descriptive prose, like poetry, may be creative, imaginative, delightful, shocking, or bizarre. But poetry is essentially metaphorical and much more work, I think, than prose.

Good poetry is crafted lean and tight. Beginning poets typically use too many words. Write, set it aside, and revisit it. Tighten it, clean it, scrub away the excess until truth is reflected clearly in its deep polish. Great commitment is required to turn unfenced prose into the finely honed metaphor we call a poem.

To poets, Shakespeare advises:

> Write till your ink be dry, and with your tears
> Moist it again, and frame some feeling line
> That may discover such integrity.

> Shakespeare
> Proteus,
> in *The Two Men of Verona*

Read your poetry aloud to hear its "music." If too many words clutter the way, they will sound like an unruly crowd. If the tune is monotonous, look for brighter words. Listen to whether it touches the soul. Well-crafted poetry seems less natural than prose in the sense of common speech, but its rhymes and rhythms are more in tune with the language and music of the heart.

The heart thinks in pictures. The soul knows truth through experience and remembers in images. Poetry paints pictures with words in a way that brings out the color and the depth of reality, opening the heart and soul. Like music and drama, it can captivate and embrace those who attend.

Poetry is a garden with flowers of every kind and description you could want, or not want, to sniff and snip and arrange in your life. It takes time to walk through this garden of graces, time to smell the various flowers and decide which suit you best.

It seems to me that fewer and fewer of the world's lovers—lovers of the beauties of life—ever get so far as the garden of poetry. Public poetry reading is nearly a lost art in Western culture. You seldom find friends and family gathering to share the latest hoot that Johnny wrote, the latest dream that Ginny set to verse. It is sad. It needs to be revived! I long for a time when poetry reading is again a respected community experience that gives pleasure and dignity to all. We've nearly lost our memory of the many graces poetry has to offer.

In thinking about Chesterton's comment (quoted earlier) that "It is the logician who seeks to get the heavens into his head. And it is his head which splits," I had to wonder, Was he thinking of Darwin? Chesterton was born six years before Darwin died (1882) and lived when Darwin's theories (and science in general) were rapidly replacing God in the mind of Western civilization.

The question came to me because of an article I had come across by Virginia Stem Owens, in which she describes the independent operational capability of the left and right hemispheres of the brain. She states that modern research would confirm Darwin's self-diagnosis that the right side of his brain atrophied due to his lifelong scientific labors. Late in his life Darwin wrote to his children:

I have said that in one respect my mind has changed during the last twenty or thirty years. Up to the age of thirty, or beyond it, poetry of many kinds . . . gave me great pleasure, and even as a schoolboy I took intense delight in Shakespeare. . . . I have also said that formerly pictures gave me considerable, and music gave me very great, delight. But now for many years I cannot endure to read a line of poetry: I have tried to read Shakespeare and found it so intolerably dull that it nauseated me. I have also almost lost any taste for pictures or music. . . . I retain some taste for fine scenery, but it does not cause me the exquisite delight which it formerly did. . . . My mind seems to have become a kind of machine for grinding general laws out of large collections of facts, but why this should have caused the atrophy of that part of the brain alone, on which the higher tastes depend, I cannot conceive. . . . The loss of these tastes is a loss of happiness, and may possibly be injurious to the intellect, and more probably to the moral charter, by enfeebling the emotional part of our nature.[4]

Darwin's story emphasizes that poetry and all forms of beauty, both man-made and God-made, bring us enjoyment and nourish the mind and soul. We stand at the end of the twenty-first century with the earlier Darwin still considered a hero of this scientific age. Our technological society is perhaps no less a half-brained (left side) enterprise than Darwin's "machine for grinding general laws out of large collections of facts." I am passionately committed to the preservation of the right brain—but hopefully, not at the expense of the left brain!

> Reason is our soul's left hand, Faith her right,
> By these we reach divinity.
>
> John Donne
> *Letter to the Countess of Bedford*, c. 1607

My passion for right brain pursuits was solidified in high school. The California State Academic Commission decided in 1968 to retroactively remove grade point credits earned for high school art and music courses from the calculation of student Grade Point Averages (GPA). The rationale: only "academic" subjects should count as college preparatory courses. Eight courses in which I had earned 4.0's were removed from my GPA. In result, I lost an opportunity for an academic scholarship to USC and was unable to go to that school.

Cultural values reflected left-brained perspectives on what was academically important and what constituted valuable intelligence. This slam on the arts in education hurt and angered me. It's part of my story that helped form my lifetime commitment to poetry, beauty, art, music, and story.

Darwin's story inspired me to write about him. What great people of different ages interest you? When you read biographies of interesting people, you enrich your knowledge for prose and poetry. What can be learned from the lives of Bach and Beethoven, Darwin and Einstein, Solzhenitsyn and Karol Wojtyla (Pope John Paul II)? People's real life stories can inspire poetry. I imagine I am the person I'm reading about and write out in a poem a picture from his/her life.

Despite my passion for the arts in general and poetry especially, I cannot teach you how to write a poem. I have described what poetry is like, how it is different from prose, and why it is important. I might even have persuaded you that poetry is essential for more evolved brains, counting on Darwin for support! But I cannot tell you how to write poetry.

Like journaling, you just have to do it. Play with it. Picture something in your mind or out of doors and describe it with wonder in the details.  Play with the details. Have fun with it.  Like picking flowers in a garden, or painting a portrait of your most beloved activity or possession, play!  That's what I do—and sometimes I find poetry is a marvelous way to talk to God.

> Your love 'round me
> an enormous yes
> clothing me in silken rejoicing
> shodding my feet with
> a ballerina's shoes and steps
> I will never prefer sensible shoes again

> Susan Paul
> Vancouver, B.C., 1995

Of course, as with any art, it helps to have good tools: a good dictionary and thesaurus, books on how to construct poetry, and books of those poets whose work you most admire will all help.

Reading for increased knowledge, as described above, is an important way to enrich yourself for poetry writing. But the best "tools" are the resources inside  of you—a heart for life in all its realities, a sense of rhythm, an ear for tone and rhyme, an eye for the world around you, and a sense of humor.

My boys will never forget the roll-on-the-floor howling laughter inspired by Roald Dahl's poems in his books *Dirty Beasts* and *Revolting Rhymes.*  His absurdity is hilarious. Another such work you and your children might enjoy is William Cole's *Ghastly Girls and Beastly Boys.*

My grandfather Jake was a natural humorist and poet.  I credit him as the source of humor in our family.  He kept us in stitches with his ironic humor that poked fun at aspects of society which he deemed ridiculous or harmful.

For example, Grandpa did not appreciate that colleges were teaching Darwin's theory of evolution as though it were fact. So he wrote a poem to help his grandchildren see how ridiculous the idea was. He would recite the following playful little with poem with such gleeful arrogance that we could believe him to be the person he spoofed—and we got his message:

The Polliwog

Once I was a polliwog
when life did first begin.
Then I was a bullfrog
with my tail tucked in.
Then I was a monkey
swinging from a tree;
Now I'm a college professor
with my Ph.D.

Jacob W. Bert
Upland, CA 1960

Besides a generous dose of humor, you will make good use of a deep well of love and a heart full of passion. Poetry yearns for love and longs for something more. Poetry grasps for the ultimate, the infinite. Write about whatever inspires your passion.

Read Milton and Shelley, Donne and Yeats, Shakespeare, of course, and Spenser, Browning and Burns. I enjoy more poets than I mention here, but the Bard said, "to thine own self be true." It would be untrue to myself not to share at least one of many beloved sonnets with you.

Shall I compare thee to a summer's day?
Thou art more lovely and more temperate.
Rough winds do shake the darling buds of May,
And summer's lease hath all too short a date.
Sometime too hot the eye of heaven shines,
And often is his gold complexion dimmed;
And every fair from fair sometime declines,
By chance, or nature's changing course, untrimmed;
But thy eternal summer shall not fade,
Nor lose possession of that fair thou ow'st,
Nor shall Death brag thou wand'rest in his shade,
When in eternal lines to time thou grow'st.
So long as men can breathe or eyes can see,
So long lives this, and this gives life to thee.

William Shakespeare
*Sonnet 18*

It is not surprising why many moderns do not think poetry is easy to understand. It is a paradox of the modern world that we have all the classics literally at our fingertips through modern technology, but we are far less literary than any preceding generation. We have information, but not understanding. As a result, many of the richest treasures of our heritage are virtually lost to us.

Spenser's famous marriage poem, *Epithalamion* (1595) for example, is a classic that experts of occasional poetry (poetry written for a certain occasion) say has never been topped. You and I, however, will understand it only if we are familiar with Greek mythology or have a reference book on the Greek gods at hand.

Similarly, Robert Burns' work is a Scottish flavor of old English that is very different from the old English of Chaucer, even more so from modern American English! It is an adventure to sort through such works to understanding, but you will find that newer editions usually provide a helpful glossary of terms for modern readers. I read the more difficult poetry when on vacation, when there is plenty of time to ponder and look up words in the dictionary, but choosing an appropriate time for poetry reading and writing is always a challenge.

The funny stuff, of course, is great to read anytime, even at the dinner table. Writing humorous poems can be done anywhere, in restaurants, in the car. There is much to see that inspires humor. Family meetings can be a good time for poetry. Bedtime is a good time for love poems—for reading them anyway. Once you have read a few you might not have time to write!

For a change of pace, take your journal, a pen, a thermos of your favorite beverage and a book of poetry to the park, and enjoy. If it's cold out, curl up in an afghan on your favorite wing-back chair with a steaming cup and a great book in hand, and indulge.

There are few times when I read poetry that my brain doesn't get in gear to write some. What I write may have nothing at all to do with what I just read, or what I read may have inspired me.

After a bath in a hot soaking tub one night, I wrote several poems after reading an article in the magazine *Victoria* by Madeleine L'Engle, one of my favorite living poets, who described (in prose) her special, secret place. Her place and her character, Mrs. Whatsit, were responsible for my inspiration:

> Life is a sonnet
>
> You're given the form
>
> and then must write
>
> your own poem.[5]

Here is one of my "bath and Whatsit" poems:

> Sometimes
> I look around
> frantic   frantic . . .
> I have no special place!
>
> Lord, where
> where
> is a little cozy corner
> with a view of course
> where I can hide my face
> and bear . . .
>
> and seeing no space
> before my eyes
> or in my home or yard
> nor at the river for the people
> are always there . . .
>
> Then you, my Lord
> remind me
> you had no place to hide
> nor to rest your head
> still, I remember
> you went off to a quiet place
> it says so in your Word
>
> Oh Jesus, thank you
> for remembering to me
> the only place I need
> I have always had
> inside of you
> inside of me
> everywhere   anywhere
> You are my secret place

Susan Paul
Richland, 1995

Read George Herbert, C.S. Lewis, G.K. Chesterton, and George MacDonald for poetry of faith. *A Widening Light, Poems of the Incarnation,* edited by Luci Shaw, is an anthology of contemporary Christian poetry. I recommend all the poetry by Luci Shaw and Madeleine L'Engle. Other poets in the anthology include Eugene H. Peterson, Chad Walsh, Mark Noll, Elizabeth Rooney, Jean Jantzen and Eugene Warren. Here's one sample from Mark Noll:

Christ's Crown

The leaves emerge—a growing
garland lying lightly on his head.
The dance of Spring, of resurrection,
quicks his feet; from all directions
caper those he'll call his own.
The sun shines warming down upon
the dancers and their pivot. Only those
up close can smell and see the thick
black-red the flowers nurse upon.[6]

This is poetry without verse. It has some rhyme, some flow, but no exact meter. When you write poetry, you are not limited to matching line by line, syllable by syllable, rhythm by rhythm. The picture you create and the meaning you intend is far more important than rhyme or meter *per se*.

Novices like myself, though, will often begin experimenting with poetry with some form in rhyme or some metered rhythm. These more familiar poetic structures help us begin composing, a little like "painting by the numbers." Whatever seems most helpful to you, you can make a start. Try to write a picture, describe your idea in an imaginative way, and see what happens.

Eight years ago, we had two lovely and exceptional young women living with our family of three boys. Among us, we represented three cultures and at least seven or eight different perspectives on everything we discussed! It was a delightful and rich time, and also had its share of misunderstanding and confusion—times when I found myself driven to poetry at the foot of the Cross.

Poetry provides a shelter of imagination for stirred emotions that are not yet sorted into clear and cogent thoughts. The Cross, where Christ suffered for us, is the picture of the end of sin and the birth of eternal life. When we saints find our experience is far from saintly, we find solace in Christ and comfort in the picture he makes for us as we address our emotions or experience in a poem.

> God's shadows we
>     though images be
>     yet reflections too poor
> His rich light unfree
>     to flow its myriad fluid color
>     through the stone-dull core
> of Christ ones such as we
>
> One light alone is sure
> His mercy flows secure
>     nailed to the shadow tree
>     runs ever its blood-sap pure
> Coloring dull, melting stone
> Lighting images with His Own
> Beckoning shadows—follow me.

Susan Paul
Richland, 1988

The poetry of the Bible moves us to contemplate who God is. According to Dan Allender and Tremper Longman in *Cry of the Soul,* "The poetry [of the Psalms] is God's invitation to glimpse the unseen, his very character." Their book has been an eye-opener for me into the Psalms as a book that tells us much about God's emotions and what they mean. I am challenged to a deeper study of my own. What would he lament, what would he rejoice over, if God wrote poetry to us today?

Try reading the Psalms out loud; better yet, sing them! Pick some of your favorites and notice the flow and balance in the sound of the verse, though there is seldom rhyme and the rhythms are not metered (at least not in English). I have tried rewriting some of David's psalms in my own words, adding a thought or two as appropriate to my own situation. Reading the Psalms may move you to create your own praise poems, and reading these aloud may bring you the same experience described here:

> *My heart is stirred by a noble theme*
> *as I recite my verses for the King;*
> *my tongue is the pen of a skillful writer.*
>
> (*Psalm 45:1*)

In the same way that relationship with God occasions praise in poetry, so a dear friend who has been generous with you can occasion affirmation through poetry.

For Laura

Delight inhabits Laura's laugh
Beauty and sweet comfort
    fruits of her hands
Delicious grace her gentle perfume
Truth roots tenderly where
    Laura plants

Susan Paul
Vancouver, B.C., 1995

The discoveries and joys of childhood and youth are great occasions for poetry. Poetry written for children may recall your own childhood. But the poetry that children write recalls discovery in a most winsome way.

Children can produce remarkable poetry if we encourage their natural imagination. I have tried to do this with my boys. My first son, Noel, has written several poems. This one, written for a school assignment, recalls sailing in the Greek Isles in June of 1994 , when he was fifteen:

A Little Dream

I shove off, leave the city there
a stranger waves from shore
The waves fall into rhythm
rocking back and forth

I pull the sheet in, catch the wind
I sail on starboard tack
back and forth back and forth
I smile, I am relaxed

A light breeze on a sea calm and grey
orange sunset before me
And the misty horizon makes
ambiguous the sky from sea

I skirt the wavelets in a tiny boat
close-hauled and by and by
alone I'll sail and think and live
forever, I will fly

The sun dips low and drops away
but now the stars I see
I sing out loud, I talk to God
I let him talk to me

The sea is tranquil, water cool
day rises fresh and fast
I look again back toward the land
my boat turn 'round at last

Noel R. Paul
Richland, 1995

Noel was inspired, at age fourteen, to go to Albania as part of a mission team by a friend who, at fourteen, had been the youngest member of a team from Fresno's First Presbyterian Church. Ashlie met five-year-old Anita at an orphanage for mentally handicapped children.

Anita
On top of a hill you lay quietly
In a cold building, far away
You were kept from society
And denied a chance in the world.
You were full of innocence—
Too young to know of evil,
Too young to know that you
Were being kept from happiness.
I saw you in a corner,
Alone and afraid.
Your eyes drew me near and
As you listened to me sing, I knew
you understood me— hope was built.
When I touched your soft face I knew
you were a gift to me; A gift of God
who was trapped in a world of ignorance.
A friendship was built as I held you
And you put your head on my shoulder.
I saw joy in your turquoise eyes
As I began to cherish my last minutes with you.
Not a word was spoken
But when I smoothed your hair
And kissed you on the forehead
Your smile showed it all.
Perhaps you may be in heaven
When I return,
But until I see you there
I will always remember
The day you became
My precious friend.

Ashlie Elizabeth Fletcher
Albania, 1992

My mother is an energetic person of many talents. She writes stories and poetry and artful letters—one of the few people I know who still gives the special gift of beautifully composed personal letters in an era that has largely forgotten the art. She has encouraged me all my life with my meager attempts at writing. I enjoy her writing and love her poetry.

Chrysanthemums...
On D.H. Laurence's short story,
"Odour of Chrysanthemums"

Disheveled pink chrysanthemums
    hung like rosy ragged cloths
    to dry, on sooty jagged strands.

Frail wan flowers
    tied like pallid fluttering moths
    to broadening apron bands.

Evening garden essence
    raptured joy in twilight
    in fragrant spicy fronds.

Tragic brown chrysanthemums
    in final deathblight
    sere, withered flower bonds.

Marylou Bert
Washington, 1992

Tangents

Ash clouds sift winter rain
My lips taste brine and sweet
    salt sorrow blends.

Hot streams shaft summer sun
My lips swerve, curve to meet
    a smile, joy sends.

Marylou Bert
Washington, 1992

Sons of Summer

One sandy shell, a brown earth rock
    crumpled papers, a rusty lock
    and words to spell,
    a pocket's store unfolds.

Levi's, torn at knees and heels
    T-shirts used to polish wheels,
    dusty sneakers, one stray sock,
    bedroom, center stage…a bat.

Eager eyes, brown bodies strong,
    Joyful voices, they belong
    to Love and Ardent Life.

Our golden sons of summer.

> Marylou Bert
> California, 1973

My own youth creeps back into view as I reread old journals of poetry and prose. Desires for identity and love echo through all ages and stages of life, but are somehow most poignant in youth.

Dream

I dream of you—my faceless love
I dream you really care
I see you only enough to know
You are in my future
      somewhere
My love for you is powerful
and yours for me, the same
How can it be then, with a love
like ours, that I don't even know
      your name?

> Suzi Bert
> Fresno, 1968

Face

You were there
when I least expected
(even dreaded)
the music to begin
inside the hall
where I kept my face,

and when you left
the face itself was gone.

                              Suzi Bert
                              Fresno, 1971


Before I wrote the first of these poems, "face" had already become a metaphor for my sense of identity, my sense of self.  Face is the opposite of "faceless."  To have a face meant to me to be a person recognized, known, and loved for who I am.

Like other adolescent girls, I sought my identity as a woman in relationships with young men.  *Dream* was written after the end of my first experience of falling in love—an expression of my hard-won acceptance that the relationship was over.  I was looking to the future.

The later poem reflects my "facelessness" after a second "love" dropped me for another young woman.  This was a more serious break-up; we had dreamed of marriage.  I feared my loss of identity might never be recovered.  The music had stopped.

This poem has resurfaced several times in my life when I have gone through a change in the definition of my sense of self.  At times, I have addressed this poem to my husband, and on occasion, even to God.

God was always there in my life. He protected me through
childhood. He made the sweet music of grace and praise
begin beautifully when I committed my face—my identity,
my whole self—to him. I expected the music of his
presence to always fill the hall—the secret place where I
reflected on my life—the anteroom between my personal
self and the personality I shared with the world. It was
he who designed a place in me which wanted intimacy
with him and he who, when the love relationship failed,
seemed to leave it empty—totally desolate.

Your own poems can be significant to you at various times
in your life, if they get at something of the real pain or joy
of the occasion that inspired them.

Reading others' poetry and novels can inspire your own
venture into poetry, and can help you expand your self-
identity. A few books have played special roles in
inspiring my poetry and my journey to define myself.

*Til We Have Faces,* by C.S. Lewis, is a novel that I intended
to read long ago because its title had fascinated me since
I discovered it after I wrote the poems quoted above. Yet
it was one book I kept myself from reading during a time
when I felt "faceless," when my identity seemed unclear
and my person unloved. The heroine of the book
struggled with her ugliness as I had struggled with mine,
and I had enough to contend with than to want to read
about an imaginary person who hurt the way I did.

In rereading the "face" poem in an old journal, I found
this entry underneath:

> The Lord has given me a face. I no longer hang it
> in the hall or put it on when I go out. It is attached.
> I had forgotten that I wanted to read *Til We Have
> Faces* now that I have my own face. But I have not
> yet read it—because I was saving it for some

special time, which signifies that in some way, I may still be looking for a face.

My identity as a woman, wife, lover, and mother was clear when I wrote this—I was loved and known as such. But I was at another point of transition and grasping for a new definition to add to my identity, which brought up the old metaphor. Soon after that journal entry, I at long last read the book and was delighted to discover that it encouraged me. My more recent poetry celebrates the new and mature sense of self that I have come to.

*The Last Battle* was another book that I put off reading for awhile after a young friend, in a moment of anger, told me that I reminded her of Susan, one of the main characters in C.S. Lewis' series, *The Chronicles of Narnia*. This was quite a devastating statement for me at that time, since the Susan of the book eventually proves unfaithful to her sister and brothers, her Lord, and herself. Was this really my "face" or even worse, my destiny?

It was not difficult to forgive Melody, who was a precocious pre-adolescent at the time, since *I* was a "mature" twenty-year-old who loved her. She did not know me well or understand the hidden sensitivity of my nature. Yet I had to force myself to start that book. In reading it, I found a way to affirm that I was not Lewis's Susan, but my *own* Susan. In fact, I was not like her, I was more like Lucy! Much more importantly, in that discovery, I felt confirmed as *Jesus' Susan*.

Most times, the poetic and passionate, sensitive nature of a person—his or her "poetic face"—is deeply hidden from others. Poetry is intensely personal and reflects the heart. It often remains the most personal and private of writings, hidden from the world. Famous poets may be exceptions because their works are not hidden, but even for many of these at an earlier time in their story, their works were hidden.

All poets have this sensitive nature and write from the heart as well as from keen powers of observation. Walt Whitman is a poet many Americans have loved whose heart was not hidden, as seen in this poem:

> I hear and behold God in every object, yet understand
>     God not in the least,
> Nor do I understand who there can be more
>     wonderful than myself.
> Why should I wish to see God better than this day?
> I see something of God each hour of the twenty-four,
>     and each moment then,
> In the faces of men and women I see God, and in my
>     own face in the glass,
> I find letters from God dropped in the street, and
>     every one is signed by God's name,
> And I leave them where they are, for I know that
>     wheresoe'er I go
> Others will punctually come forever and ever.[7]

Whitman was a great poet and observer of nature. Though he tipped his hat to the God he saw reflected in creation, as far as we know he never showed much interest in God beyond that. For Whitman there was no one more wonderful than himself.

You will find Walt Whitman quoted in journals and prose books saying, "The best gift you can give is a portion of your self." This might be true if you have nothing to give your *whole* self to. Poetry can be a powerfully persuasive in pointing people to give themselves to something, to care for something they had not thought to care for before.

It has been said that the writers, poets and philosophers have more influence on the attitudes of society than all other professions put together. I do not know if this is true of our world as much as it was in past ages when the arts were more celebrated in education and in life. But I do believe Walt Whitman has had a profound influence philosophically on American culture. His godlessness has influenced many to celebrate God's creation without celebrating God.

My dear friend, Isabelle Goddard, who helped me find my "face" in Christ, did Walt Whitman one better on the subject of giving one's self:

> The only thing we can really give God is our right to ourselves.
>
> Isabelle Goddard
> Nanteuil-les-Meaux, 1991

Poets who celebrate God's creation can influence us to care about the earth and our environment. People that celebrate God himself, like Isabelle, powerfully influence others to care about the whole creation, including the people.

A life wholly given to something can inspire poetry and prose. Isabelle's life is wholly given to the Lord Jesus. She has inspired me in many ways, including poetry and I will always love her "face"—the inner person she is that she gives to the people in her worlds. I am grateful for the hope and earthy reality of her influence. This prose from her journal mirrors her gift of her whole self and the effect on her life.

> *According to my earnest expectation and my hope, that in nothing I shall be ashamed, but that with all boldness, as always, so now also Christ shall be magnified in my body, whether it be by life, or by death.*
>
> *(Phil .1:20 KJV)*

When I was nineteen, I knew I was a dumpy, plain person. I chose this verse to live my life by, and it has been a wonderful, amazing life!

Isabelle Goddard
Richland, 1995

Your poems represent what you give your heart to, and through them, you may discover what you want to live your life by. They will tell you about your own "face" in the way I have described it—your identity. They will tell you what your identity taps into—what things of life carry meaning for you.

Most of us talk about wanting to mature as we grow older. I call this process "adding to my identity, building and renewing my sense of self." Poetry helps me to do this. I revel in discovering how much certain things, people and experiences matter to me as they come forth in new poems, or in phrases that may become poems and must be set to paper before they evaporate.

Through poetry, the deep emotions of your heart, the central desires of your inner self, can come out. Your poems may reflect what you abhor. I encourage you to use this genre of personal writing to explore that, too.

What do you detest? Write a poem about it. How much are you like God in hating all that is evil, tragic, sinful and hurtful to humanity? How would you best lament what grieves you—in prose or poetry? And what do you celebrate? What causes your heart to sing and your body to want to dance? Would a poem say it better than a bit of prose?

If you have written *any* poetry or prose at any time in the past, dig it out and read it. Find a way to write what you see now, and how you see differently than before. What will you discover about your search for your "face"—your identity? How has God revealed his face to you? What new understanding of how God has nourished your life can you uncover? Does celebrating God's world cause you to celebrate him as well?

Poetry and prose can be delightful, imaginative, dramatic, sometimes sheltering ways to write myriad pieces of your story. But as Natalie Goldberg says, "We are not the poem. There is no permanent truth [about yourself or anything] you can corner in a poem that will satisfy you forever."[8] No single poem nor a whole life's collection of poetry or prose can describe all of who you are. This is part of the joy of poetry to me, it can never reveal all, but it reveals a piece of the puzzle of who we are, painting graphic pictures that yield new perspectives in colors and hues that may not come forth in any other way. As you experiment and play with poetry, some pictures you words paint will reveal metaphors that become meaningful to you because they illumine your identity, expand your perspective, or mirror the reality of your circumstances and reflect fresh insight.

You matter. Your story matters. *Enjoy* playing with poetry.

# Chapter 4

# Story Writing:
# A Story You Create

"It was much pleasanter at home," thought poor Alice, "when one wasn't always growing larger and smaller, and being ordered about by mice and rabbits. I almost wish I hadn't gone down that rabbit hole; and yet—and yet—it's rather curious you know, this sort of life! I do wonder what can have happened to me! When I used to read fairy tales I fancied that kind of thing never happened, and now here I am in the middle of one! There ought to be a book written about me, that there ought! And when I grow up I'll write one—"

Lewis Carroll
Alice,
in *Alice in Wonderland*

Story writing is something many people imagine doing and talk about doing—but despite the plethora of books on the shelves, few actually do. I would like to see that change.

Story writing can be many things (see Glossary), but I will focus here and in the next chapter on forms that suit my purpose—to help you value your own story. We will look at story writing as a means of self expression, responding to life and honoring God or whatever you want to honor. In this chapter I focus on creative fiction writing—a story you create. In the next chapter we will look at one form of creative non-fiction—personal and family history writing.

I describe both these kinds of story writing as a dialogue with life. You will find that writing a fiction story that comes out of your imagination is like talking to yourself. You will see yourself in the story, and you will dialogue with the story as to where it is going, how it is going to get there and what it is ultimately going to say.

With a family history or your own biography, it is your story, your life, and again, in the writing of it, you will find yourself dialoguing with yourself, your family and relatives and friends, with the life you have lived so far. In both cases, it is a dialogue that has meaning, is creative and will prove immensely satisfying.

As with poetry and prose, you must be a reader of stories if you hope to be a writer of stories. As you read this chapter, think about what kinds of stories you like to read, and what stories you have read that have influenced you.

The stories we read in childhood have a tremendous effect on our lives. Alice and I were friends. I must have read her adventures at least three times before I was a teen. And I agreed with her that home was a pleasanter place. I loved to read and write at home as a child. For one thing, you could eat and drink while reading and writing, something they would never allow at school!

Great books read at home make home a place of delightful adventure for children. My own beginnings in writing stories came early, at home, as I was read to by my mother and enjoyed reading myself. Robert Louis Stevenson's books and poetry, *Grimm's Fairy Tales*, and a large anthology of children's stories and poetry, the *Madeline* books by Louis Bemelmans, *Mother Goose*, the *Oz* stories by Frank Baum, the fables by Oscar Wilde, and of course, the *Adventures of Alice* and *Through the Looking-Glass* by Lewis Carroll, were all constant companions.

In grade school and at home, I wrote many stories about family, inspired by the books of Beverly Cleary, A.A. Milne, Laura Ingles Wilder, and the classics *Cheaper by the Dozen* by Frank Gilbreth, and *The Secret Garden* and *Little Lord Fauntleroy* by Frances Hodgson Burnett.

I regret that one day I burned every childhood story of my own that I could find in a fit of shame and self-hatred. I don't remember the occasion—I had probably just done something horrible to my brother and received my just dues, a spanking. But self-punishment was needless and destructive. I remember watching the stories burn in the huge, rusty, old-fashioned incinerator in the alleyway behind our small house in Brawley, California. As the stack of pages turned to ashes before my eyes, I knew that someday I would be sorry. Ah, the consequences of being a dramatic child of nine!

It was not long after that occasion that I began writing again—and determined never again to burn my stories. But I have kept them hidden. They were mine, and they were for *my* pleasure. I determined never to take them more seriously than that. You see, unlike Alice, I had not the confidence to think there ought to be a book about me, much less that I could grow up and really write it myself. I did not know then that I mattered or that my story could matter that much.

Story writing is a very personal thing. You will find a lot of yourself coming out on the pages as the pen or pencil or keyboard flies, even though you are describing the heroine or her mother, or the scenery. Whatever the problem is that needs answering, whatever the mystery is that needs solving, whatever the adventure that needs living out, you will find yourself in it. A good description of the personal nature of writing can be found in Marjorie Williams' book, *Writing Articles for the Heart*, as well as some excellent tips for how to go about characterization, dialogue and setting. Here is one of my favorite tips, from Ernest Hemingway:

There is no rule on how it is to write. Sometimes it comes easily and perfectly. Sometimes it is like drilling rock and blasting it out with charges.[1]

Writing will happen if you have the desire and give it freedom. I mentioned "the flow" of writing in the chapter on journaling. The same experience can happen writing a story.

People who love to write often discover this amazing experience, though they describe it somewhat differently. It is, however, the same experience. I call it the Spirit connecting my heart and mind to my hand and giving me the story. When this happens, the writing flows from the pen or through the finger tips onto keys with almost no effort, the way a great pianist seems effortlessly to make music flow from his soul into a room. It simply must come out.

Two of my favorite writers, Henri Nouwen and Madeleine L'Engle, describe it this way:

> It is a remarkable sensation to see ideas and words flowing so easily, as if they had always been there, waiting.[2]

> We cannot create until we acknowledge our createdness... An artist is a nourisher and a creator who knows that during the act of creation there is collaboration. We do not create alone.[3]

> The artist cannot manage the normalcy [of stark journalism]. Vision keeps breaking through, and must find means of expression.[4]

Madeleine L'Engle's stories have been favorites of my son Noel, as well as mine. To me, her works rank with those of C.S. Lewis, George MacDonald, Charles Williams, G.K.

Chesterton and Elizabeth Goudge. She knows the Creator and serves the art he gives her even as these other great authors did. In *Walking on Water*, L'Engle describes the art of creating as "serving the art that is given," and gets at the heart of the profound paradox in the creative process.

> During the creation of any form of art, art which affirms the value and holiness of life, the artist must die. To serve a work of art, great or small, is to die, to die to self.[5]

She describes this death to self as a part of the artist's collaboration with the Creator in the process of creation. She says it is similar to the contemplative saint's "prayer of the heart," which turns inward not to find self, but to lose self in order to be found by God. One must let go of, lose, die to self in order to find the art—in our case, the story.

If you lose yourself to the Creator and the story he gives you as you write, you will experience a total lack of self-absorption and the story will flow out of you, as if it was always there waiting. Then, as you read what is there, you will both know and be known by the story that comes out. You will see yourself somehow. The collaborator, the Creator, has used what is in you and what you have experienced in life or through reading to create the story. It is because we see ourselves in our stories that we can either delight to share them and try to see them given out or published, or dare not show them to anyone. What if they don't really honor God?

What kind of story is acceptable for a Christian to write? I hear many people say that they would love to write children's books, and to be sure, we could use more Christians writing them. I often wish, when reading magazines and newspapers and journals (medical and educational journals are fascinating!), that the authors were Christians. How different would the articles be? A practiced and discerning reader will suspect who the Christian cartoonists, journalists and authors are long before it is revealed explicitly, because of a difference in philosophy and values. Is the story life-nurturing or life-draining?

Do you think that a fictitious story must be about someone seeking Jesus and finding him in order to be a work that honors him? Some Christians do. I'm not one of them.

It dismays me that great art is sometimes disparaged by people who claim to know the Master Creator just because the artist did not believe in God—as if lack of faith in God could cancel out the gift of creativity he has given! Conversely, it saddens me that the fine art of Christians is sometimes disparaged because the artist dares to make his or her faith public, as though *faith* disqualifies one as an artist! I experience God's glory and his Spirit's presence in amazing ways through many great works of art—visual, musical, dramatic, written—regardless of the artist's personal knowledge of God or intent to honor him.

My friend Sarah Meekhof values the potential of stories to reinforce positive values and give good fun to small children. She is creating children's stories, which she hopes to publish. Sarah desires to see more life-nurturing books that encourage imagination and bring hope into homes of those who don't yet know Jesus, as well as to those who do. I pray that her hope will be realized, for God is being honored already in her creativity.

> Animals speak their own language, it's true;
> Oh! the things they would say if only we knew—
> But if you think it's silly, what animals may say,
> Just listen to what YOU are saying some day!

Sarah Meekhof
*excerpt from a preschool story*

Creativity that values life, beauty and all that is good and pleasant, and that knows the reality of sin's results—human wretchedness and suffering—honors the God who made the beauty and redeems the wretchedness. I believe that art, motivated by love, honors the Creator. We are created by his love, and we are recreated by his love as new creations, through his death and through our own suffering as well. Margery Williams captures this profound truth with great winsomeness in her well-loved book, *The Velveteen Rabbit:*

> The Skin Horse said, "The Boy's Uncle made me Real. . . once you become Real, you can't become unreal again. It lasts for always."
>
> The rabbit sighed. He longed to become Real, to know what it felt like; and yet the idea of growing shabby and losing eyes and whiskers was rather sad. He wished that he could become it without these uncomfortable things happening to him.[6]

Uncomfortable things happen in life, in story and in the creative process. This creative process and its discomforts are always somewhat of a mystery. One sculpture in the famous series by Michelangelo, *Out of the Stone*, reminds me of the mystery and struggle of the times when a writer does not experience the "flow." When the next step in the story just doesn't come forth, it might as well be in stone.

In Florence, you can view this series, and it is fascinating. There are six or seven sculptures in the series, and each one depicts a man struggling to be released from an eight-foot stone. Part of what is fascinating to me is that Michelangelo created them in what we might think is reverse order. The one most fully revealed has only a small portion of his back and one heel still attached to the marble slab behind him that has been chiseled away. He is in a running posture and seems most youthful of the men in the series. One knee is raised and he looks poised to leap out. He has an expression of joyous anticipation on his up-raised face.

In each successive sculpture the man is more deeply embedded in his slab of marble. Each one seems a little older. It is uncertain, but I had the impression that it could be the same man. There is less joy and more struggle implied in each successive man's posture and facial expression.

The last slab is a whole marble pillar almost untouched by the sculptor's chisel. The man inside has only the tip of a nose, a frowning brow and forehead protruding about half-way down the pillar of marble. He must be bent, bowed by the weight of the stone above him. He is trying to stand as well as break free. A right palm pushes up above the head out of the stone, a bit of the left elbow jabs out of one side. A left foot thrusts out and the right knee cap juts out, low to the ground. When I saw it, I had a sense that the person in stone was pressed down and suffocating. He was dying to move, aching to live, miserable in the binding marble and desperate to break free, stand up and move.

For me, Michelangelo's *Out of the Stone* series is a metaphor for writing a story. When the "flow" is there, the writing runs across the page like the runner. When the "flow" stops, and the writer gets stuck, the story is like the man in the last stone pillar, embedded in a mysterious block from which he cannot escape on his own. Instead the writer must work, be disciplined, and keep chipping away until he frees the story, his work of art, out of the stone.

Phyllis A. Whitney, in *Guide to Fiction Writing*,[7] describes the process of writing as either venturesome—just write it, or consistent—plan it and have a plan for the times when a "block" comes, or as I call it, when you hit stone. In the venturesome approach, you may not know all the characters who are going to show up in the story, nor where the story is going to go. With the consistent approach, you set forth a plan, stick to it and have an alternative plan for doing something else connected to the writing process, like some more research or some cataloging of your bibliography or end notes, until you have a sense that some inspiration is returning.

With either process, discipline will come in to it if you want your story to be real. It will take work to get it out of the stone of not knowing what is next. It will take perseverance to get the story onto paper that gives it a place to live and become real. I sensed that Michelangelo's muscular figure, once freed to break out of stone, would somehow become real, like the velveteen rabbit or Pinocchio, because of the love of the sculptor. In the same way Michelangelo loved the man enough to show his story in sculpture, you must love your story in order to access the discipline to keep chipping away at it.

A story will not become real, that is, alive, an imitation of life so alive that it seems real, even to the writer, without this discipline of keeping at it. This takes the commitment of love. I know this because I have several stories waiting to be freed out of stone. Somewhere in each story, at some time in my life, I stopped loving the story enough to keep at it. Each of these stories is stuck in a different stage of being revealed and becoming real. One is virtually alive now—it is in my head almost all the time.

There are some basic elements to a story that are important to know to help you get started. First off, you need a character and a problem or obstacle. Secondly, you need a culture, a setting, and a time in history. Thirdly, you need a direction or a plot; that is, what happens to the character and what is she/he doing about it? Finally, you need a climax, a solution, and a final discovery, the thing learned or achieved by the character. I recommend Whitney's book, and there are many others, that will give you helpful suggestions for how to develop each of these parts to a story.

The most important thing I can tell you is that you must *believe* in the story. It must be true—not true in the sense of factual—but true to life, real. The dialogues, the personalities of the characters, the setting, the action—everything must be so believable that it tells truth about humanity, the human condition. You must believe it, or you will not finish it. This, indeed, is why many of the stories I have written over the last twenty years are still in stone. Somewhere or other, they became unbelievable to me. Too idealistic, too sympathetic or saccharine, too depressing, too unreal!

People have asked me how to make the characters believable. Make them like the real people you know and read about. But mix up the qualities enough so that your friends don't exactly recognize themselves. Or use a pseudonym! All of us have some good qualities and some flawed ones. Plastic characters with no flaws, cardboard cutout characters with no good points except perhaps brains or beauty, come in droves off the tabloid and pulp fiction shelves.

A friend told me she felt damaged by the pulp fiction she read to help her learn English when she came from Germany to study at an American university. It was so unrealistic about the love relationship between a man and woman that she was disappointed with every real man she dated. Make your characters realistic enough to be flawed somehow and they will be more real to you and to the reader. And they will not set up the gullible reader to be disappointed with reality!

I judged my own work as unbelievable, even when my characters had flaws and good points. It was a mistake that solidified the stone. Now it would be such tremendous work to return to those stories and bring them to life again. I find it much more delightful to begin a new story than to try to recover from stone the story of people who once "lived" in my head. And it is easier to apply the discipline of keeping at it with the current story than with an "old" one.

Do not judge your writing, especially not while you work. Go ahead and do whatever planning you can do about where you want your story to go. Go there, and certainly, revise when what comes onto the paper is not what you meant to say. If you cannot go there, make a new plan based on where your characters seem to want to go instead. Judge the words on the page in so far as they are congruent with your meaning, or a dialogue as to whether or not it gets your character to where she wants to go next. But do not judge the whole work, the whole plot, the whole chapter, the whole anything!

As I emphasized in the journaling chapter, and I cannot stress enough that judgment is destructive to creativity. Look what shame and judgment did to the little girl's stories that her adult self would have loved to read! In my own fiction writing, I am a better negative example than a positive one, but it is still true to my story at this time.

The adventure for my story writing ahead is unclear, perhaps improbable, but not impossible. Maybe I can keep chipping away at the one story that is virtually real in my mind. The characters live for me. It is so much fun to get to know them. They remind me of many real friends and acquaintances from past times and places in my life. Because they live for me, I want them to go somewhere life-nurturing. I want my story to honor life, to honor some values I hold dear in relationships like loyalty, which seems to have been lost to current American vocabulary and lifestyle. I would be very pleased if I could feel my stories honored Jesus and his gracious love for all people in some way.

I do not want to cast the characters of my current story in the stone of judgment and let them die. If they live, maybe the story will move to its conclusion, and maybe it will be true enough to someone else that it could be publishable. What will happen? Only God knows!

I would love to find in some cob-webbed attic trunk a story that my great-grandmother had written that would help me know her a little more! I hope to finish my story because I imagine that a niece or granddaughter might enjoy reading it someday.

You can use your creative fiction to honor whatever you value, whether it is the Lord Jesus, or Bhudda, Nietzche or David Letterman. Your story will reflect something of what you like and don't like even if you do not intend to honor anything. What you value will come through, be it the family, or horses, motorcycles, quilts, vegetable gardens or baseball cards.

Your fiction, like your poetry, will express something of who you are, not the whole of you, but some prismic perspectives. You can tell a truthful story, funny, sad, tragic, or over-coming, your story can reflect reality. You can encourage some life-nurturing values you want your grandchildren to catch. And what fun in the process!

Have at it! What kind of stories can you, with your imagination, create? If you believe in God's presence in your life, what kind of stories can you and he create together?

You matter. Your story matters, even if it comes out of your imagination and through your hands onto the page. For surely your heart, your experience and your desires will be expressed there.

# Chapter 5

# Personal and Family History Writing: A Dialogue with Life

Communication is a miracle.

Isabelle M. Goddard
Fresno, 1970

Communication *is* a miracle. True communication of essential meaning and on-target understanding from person to person is perhaps the most difficult to achieve within our families and from one generation to the next. But it is not easily achieved anywhere. It takes work.

In family life, dialogue is sometimes difficult to start, much less maintain. Whenever communication happens in our family, I count it a miracle and thank God for it.

Family meetings go a long way in our family to create a dialogue that includes us all. Anyone can call them; usually I do, or Bob, my husband, does. I am waiting for the children to catch on that they have just as much authority in the family to call for a dialogue. But true to human nature, children don't usually feel the need to value what they already have, so ours will surprise me if they actually do ever call for a Family Council. Whether they value them now or not, someday our boys will have cause to be grateful that we got together to talk things through. Working at communication is a part of their history that we are creating as we go.

Writing down who we are—where we come from, what our life has been like and what it is right now—is invaluable in creating new dialogues among families, friends and future generations. Writing your autobiography or your family history will create in you and between you and your loved ones a dialogue with life.

I hear people say they hate to write about themselves and they'd never attempt to write about their family or it's history. They are convinced that writing to create a dialogue with life would not be worth the work. In the first case, they don't like telling their own story, fearing it will be too dull, too self-focused or too commonplace. The family history idea is even more daunting. Who has the authority, after all, to view everyone in the family and make the judgments of what is put in and what is left out? The whole idea of researching, interviewing, tracking down lost relatives, finding photos and identifying everyone—it all looks like too much work.

Forget all those ideas. Celebrate the ordinary! In the ordinary you will find something of extraordinary value to you. What may seem dull or commonplace to your will look uncommon and curiously fascinating to your grandchildren or great-grandchildren.

If you have never written a biography, start small and practical. You can write about yourself, in fact, you already have done so, if you have ever worked. You have a job resumé. If you do not have a resumé, begin the story of your life with this. Start by writing down your job history—every job you have ever had, for money or not, including jobs in your childhood and what skills you learned in the process. Sooner or later you may have use for a thorough job or skills resumé, one that helps you catalog the great variety of skills you possess.

Your employment history is a big piece of your story if you are employed. It is a part of your story that is already known by others—it is probably one of the things you talk about, part of your on-going dialogue with life.

But life is more than employed work—or is it? My sister-in-law, Elena, during her residency in Virginia, has said that the biggest challenge in medical school is to "get a life!" Medical school is notorious for consuming personal life, as are all the professions. Reflect upon your work, and the variety of types of employment that you may have had. What kinds of jobs were more meaningful to you? Write down your reflections on the value and satisfaction to you personally of your jobs up to and including the present. What kinds have been most aggravating or dull? Are you at a point in your life that job satisfaction needs to increase in order to make it worthwhile to stay in that position? Write down your responses.

Sometimes, the simple task of taking stock of one's resumé and one's current job satisfaction can be very helpful in clarifying an unattended need, or a sense of fulfillment that was buried in the business of life that is party of your story right now. Write down what you were grateful for, what you got the biggest thrill from, and what depressed you the most about various jobs you have had or have now. Focusing on these kinds of questions, related to the things on which you have spent a large part of your days will move you down the road to writing your own story.

Today's collegians say that student life is only more than classes and studies if they have made friends. In many large universities, students report that few close friends are found. Listening to collegians talk about campus life, it sounds as if the larger dialogue about life that should be happening in the classrooms and informally on campus has become an endangered species. College at the end of the 20th century seems to be about "getting a job" instead of getting a life.

Reflect upon your schooling. Write down the kinds of schools you went to, how much education you had or are having now, and what subjects of study you have enjoyed most and least, what subjects you wish you had studied that you haven't. How important is education and knowledge to you? What kinds of knowledge matter to you? Have you educated yourself in ways that formal education never did? What kinds of subjects? Reflect and write about what you have loved learning in any academic or educational environment.

Do you have further educational goals or desires? Write them all down. Make a wish list! What kind of education would you just love to have if you could have all you wanted out of that aspect of life? Write it all down, set these things aside for a while and then come back to them. Are any of those desires or goals pulling your heart strings? Or do they reflect dead dreams or unrealistic ideals? What would be more realistic? Sometimes we need to get more of an education to feel we are getting more of a life that is true to who we are and want to be.

It is difficult to "get a life" without friends. To have a dialogue means to communicate in the context of a relationship. Most women who take a job outside the home, or go back to school, report that they have little or no time for friendships compared to what they had before. One might think that men, with many more decades of experience in the workplace than most women, would have learned to build a few real friendships in that context. However, the recent popularity of the Promise Keeper's men's movement suggests that men do not find satisfying friendships in the workplace any more than women, and perhaps less.

My sister-in-law, Joni, told me that when she became a mother and stopped working at the bank, friendships which existed in that setting slowly faded away. In the workplace there is often little time to dialogue about your life beyond work, or to build relationships with enough depth to survive outside that context.

Many people merely survive their work week in order to "live" on weekends. Others say they have no life, only work. My friend in Paris, Marielle Gérard, a Personnel Benefits specialist, says that Parisians describe their days by the slang phrase *metro, boulot, dodo*. Commuting, working and sleeping devour all the time there is, every day. The phrase describes a way of life with no time for friendships, little time for family, and very little time to reflect about anything—an intensely felt irony in French culture, legendary for its reflective thinkers.

The story of your life includes every part of your life, not just work or school. Your personality, your daily home life, and your future dreams define the larger and truer picture of who you are and who you are becoming. Writing down your own story will help you to see the life you've got from new eyes.

Your story is not just a collection of facts. It communicates something of who you are and what you have valued and learned in life. The same is true for stories of your parents, grandparents or ancestors. This is the nature of story, to communicate not merely facts, but truth.

> There is a prevalent illusion that nonfiction is factual and objective, and that when we read history we can find out what really happened. Not so. My mother was a southerner and my father was a damn-yankee, and I got two totally different versions of "the wa-ah," as Mother called what my father referred to as the Civil War. It's two different wars, depending on the point of view. After the "wa-ah" all anybody in my mother's family had was story.[1]

Exceptional or devastating times highlight the value of our stories and clarify what matters to us. Usually what matters most is relationships with those we love and the stories of each other's lives.

There is much to be derived from writing the history of your family: joy from the exceptional times, healing and comfort from the devastating times, a sense of humor about life and a deepened sense of appreciation about what matters to you. A number of approaches are possible to recording your history: your own story (autobiography), or a story about a parent or grandparent (biography), or about where your family came from (biographical history).

If you have never written autobiographically, start small. Start with good memories of your childhood or of some influential experience or person in your life. Or begin by describing things that come to mind from an especially hard time in your life. What happened? How did you feel? How did it change you? How is your perspective on life different because of the experience?

Try writing a description of a day in your life right now. Write one of a day in your life ten or twenty years ago. Write about an ordinary day in your childhood. Try describing your personality as a child, and as a teen. Think of a formative turning point in your maturing process; what happened and how did you change? Write it down.

How is your personality different because of major things that have happened in your story? Marriage, childbirth, death of grandparents, parents or siblings, distance moves, job changes, health problems—all these can effect changes in our lives. Write something you remember about each major event. Try to keep your writing per subject to two or three paragraphs minimum or two or three pages, maximum. Even a catalog style of writing a paragraph or two on each major event of your life as a beginning can become the basis of a very thorough autobiography later.

Your family history places your story in a context that gives meaning and scope to your life. Try writing a two or three paragraph description of each grandparent you knew, and each aunt and uncle, then cousins. Then take your parents and siblings and do the same. You will probably find that it is actually hard to stick to two paragraphs for people you know well. Try to capture how they impressed you at an early age in one, and how you feel about them at this point in your life for the second paragraph.

This could be a beginning of a little love affair. You may surprise yourself in discovering that you actually enjoy all these ordinary, unique, special individuals that make up your family tree. Think about some colorful, heroic or notorious family member of the past. What can you write about what you have heard of that person? What member of your family had the most relish in retelling that person's story? Why? Write down your perspective. Don't worry about whether it is accurate to the letter or the minute, it is your perspective.

Who were your grandparents' and parents' heroes? Who are yours? Who were your heroes in childhood? How have heroes affected the members of your family, including you? Did any of you know your heroes personally? Write it down. If you do, you will have come another step in writing the context of your own story and addressing the beginnings of a family history.

After you have recorded a few such stories, you will find that more memories float to the surface, and some may crash in on you. In any case, as the memories come "up" write them down. Write the questions that come with them. Soon you will develop curiosity to learn more and may want to begin a dialogue with family and relatives.

A family history, or your own biography, or that of your parent or grandparent is a story of your life that includes your roots, heritage, the original culture from which your family came. Family history or even the story of one antecedent can impart an inheritance to you and a legacy to your children and grandchildren. What was the character of your family? What did your ancestors do for a living? Did your ancestors believe in God? How did that affect their lives and yours?

Writing your own story, particularly the story of your childhood, can inspire interest in your parents' and grandparents' stories. My mother began writing the story of her father's life several years ago. She decided to do this after writing a few stories of her childhood growing up in India, at a British boarding school in Darjeeling. Mother began her journey to retrieve Grandfather's story with a plane ticket, a tape recorder and several empty cassette tapes. She sat with Grandpa and asked him to tell her the stories she had heard many times before, and others she had not heard about his life in India. He was a missionary there for some forty years. She turned the taped stories into written ones and gave them as gifts to all the grandchildren.

The story goes on. The Brethren in Christ Church that sent Grandpa to India became interested in his story as well, and asked my Aunt Ardys to write it. My mother shared her work with her sister and at Grandpa's 99th birthday they got together to celebrate and to further collaborate on his story. I look forward to what will be produced that can not only honor my grandfather but bless my children and grandchildren someday.

I promised to tell you the story behind my name. I was named for three women: two great-grandmothers (both Susans) and my paternal grandmother (Irene). The quilt that Great-grandmother Susan Page Bert made for my grandparents' wedding hangs in my kitchen dinette. She was a quilter—that was all I knew of her until recently. My father says they named me for her "because she was a fine Christian lady, and a good mother.  We loved her and wanted to honor her."

I asked my mother why I was named for Great-grandmother Susan Engle.  Mother said, "Grandmother Susan was uncommunicative and not very warm!"  Why was I named for her, then?  "Not so much because of who she was, although I respected her, but because I liked her *name*.  Susan seemed an 'integrious' name."

"Integrious" is not an official word in the dictionary, but Mother and I use it.  It means to us that the person has integrity—an integrated person whose words and actions match.  Mother said Great-Grandmother was a woman of integrity and personal strength, and she hoped for those qualities for me.

I would love to know more of those two Susans.  What were they like?   I do not know their stories much at all, but our discussion recalled to Mother a memory of her Grandfather Eyre:

> He was a warm, communicative, laughing man with bright blue eyes.  He often smelled like a goat!  Funny that I should remember that!  I should get these memories down on paper.

I heartily agree.  It is true, too, that our noses remember.  Certain smells will take us right back to some time and place and the feelings involved.  I am in the process of following in my mother's footsteps, tape-recording the memories my father has of his childhood and life's work.  It is a treasure.  I hope that my mother may yet record more about the personalities and stories of her grandparents and parents—I value this for me and my children.

I am grateful that I knew the other woman for whom I was named, my grandmother Hazel Irene Bert.  She was my closest grandmother whom I knew all my childhood. I know some stories of her life and I remember her well: her humor, her great farm-fresh cooking, her sparkly, dark piercing eyes that saw right through to your heart and soul, her worried "tsch tsch," and her laugh, which rang out strong and delightful. She was a woman of prayer, a woman who loved her God and her family first.

A few months after our second son Alex was born, I drove to Upland, California from Fresno, to introduce him to her. He was born on her birthday, and we had chosen her husband's name, Jacob, for his middle name. Grandpa Jake was already in heaven at the time and I wanted to give her a gift by letting her know Alex early in his life. But Grandma gave me a great and unexpected gift when I presented Alexander Jacob into her arms:

> Your great-great-grandfather and mother made a point of praying for the next five generations of their family to all know Jesus Christ as their Savior and Lord. *This* generation [she lifted Alex up a bit] is not covered by their prayers. Your grandfather and I have continued a five generation coverage in prayer for the family. I will not live much longer, maybe a few years. . . I long to be with Jake and the Lord. You must now take on the prayer for the *next* five generations—the five below you. Then your sons will be covered by five generations of prayer for them, and the next four after them. The Lord promised blessing or curse on the next four generations of those who trusted or denied Him, so your ancestors prayed for the next *five*!  [She had a twinkle in her eye, as if to say, "Weren't they wise?"] The Lord also promised to be faithful to a thousand generations of those who trust in Him. This is to become *your* prayer.

This mantle of prayer on me profoundly affects me, and the prayer coverage deeply enriches my family and my

sense of who we are. To my knowledge, like her mother
before her, Hazel's own story was not written down. Her
personality, her interests, her unique journey with God
could be forgotten. This would be tragic, since I believe
it is her prayers that have helped cover all her descendants
with God's grace. Grandma's and Grandpa's prayers
played an important part in bringing us to our own faith
in Christ. It will be a challenge and a joy to see that her
story is not lost—this bit of prose was a beginning.

A mantle of prayer—this phrase is now a part of my
family's vocabulary. Special words and phrases that carry
meaning and signify closeness and love from one
generation to the next are a precious part of our stories.

Family language, though, like the non-word "integrious,"
needs decoding when used outside the family. I find it
heartening to recognize that such a word exists in our
vocabulary (even if others tease me for using a non-word).
I celebrate the evidence of a special family language that
is living in a culture where the phenomenon of oral history
seems to be dying.

A unique family vocabulary is such an enjoyable part of
the dialogue of life that I hope the tide will change. Family
language can include nicknames, familiar stories, jokes,
poems, songs and verbal games. My husband's maternal
grandmother, Iva Pengra, had the most hilarious
expressions, like "Oh, for crying in the sink!" and "That
would scare the hairs off a brass monkey!" Where she
got these phrases remains a family mystery! Grandma
was a natural humorist, a quilter of beautiful quilts, and
an avid baseball fan (with a memory for baseball trivia
that rivaled any man's!).

Your family's oral history can be the source of much
memory-making and pleasure. One of my favorites is the
word "bofting," coined by our youngest son, Aaron. One
day when our three boys were a little younger, they and my

husband, Bob, and I were all giggling and tickling and generally enjoying a friendly wrestle together on our bed. I commented, laughing, that we were "bonding" (such a clinical term!). Aaron retorted that the experience, full of pillows and blankets and such, was much too soft for such a "hard" word, and therefore announced that we were "bofting." He defined it as "soft family bonding." His invention was an instant hit, and has become a permanent part of the Paul family vocabulary—shorthand that reminds us of warm and wonderful moments together.

Recording the funny phrases and coined words in your family is a way to value your story at the root level. What is your oral history from your childhood home? Your grandparents' homes? What kind of oral history are you creating now?

Family mealtime is one of the most important occasions for creating a positive, life-nurturing oral history. Mealtime is usually crucial for daily communication as well. Higher SAT scores have been traced to homes that have family meals together *at least once a week!* The decline of family meal times in our culture is linked with the decline of vocabulary, literacy, intelligence, and academic performance. The decline of familial oral history also may be linked to the decline of family. If we don't talk to each other and don't listen to each other, we cannot know one another's stories on any deeper level, and we thereby diminish our enjoyment of each other and the warmth of family relationships.

One of our games around the table when the children were younger was the "imitation game." If one child was whining, we would all become "whiners" until we were laughing and the whining disappeared. If one person is overly enthusiastic, the particular expression becomes a magnet for good-natured imitation, again causing us to laugh and enjoy each other. I have been accused of being overly-positive and enthusiastic. Marielle from France, who lived with us and has become a part of our extended family, says the French think all Americans are "over-affirmers." I just smile and say, "Yes, perhaps so, and that is why *you* love us!"

Cultural exchange in the home is another great treasure in our family story that has enriched our oral tradition. We love to share our home and lives with people from other cultures, and learn from them. Learning the names of animals in French (funny-sounding to our ears) with Marielle, or learning from Caroline Kirschleger that French schoolchildren study a national history that goes back over two thousand years, or learning some of the words in French, German, Spanish and Albanian which it is important *not* to mispronounce—all of these have added immeasurably to the richness of our shared experiences—and therefore history—as a family.

It is a big job to record a family history. Besides my mother, I know only a few others who are making this effort. My friend Anna Waltar is one such valiant soul. She and her husband Alan have had the opportunity to do a lot of traveling in recent years and have managed to get to Finland, where Alan's family came from.

Anna said Alan was like a delighted child discovering family locations and some living relatives in a farming region near Isokyro, where his ancestors came from. In Isokyro, they found the gravesite of his great-great-grandfather, who lived between 1828-1913. The result of a visit with some second cousins was a lovely letter and a four-generation photograph that includes Alan's great-great-grandmother. Anna is delighted, and I am delighted for her. Her sleuthing has paid off!

Anna is also trying to tackle the huge job of tracing her own roots and building a written history of her own family. It is a large family, she says, and as yet she has not discovered the connection across the ocean. But she reports excitement and joy in the discoveries along the way:

> I hope it will mean something to my children and grandchildren someday. Right now everyone is so involved in their own lives . . . but someday, I think it will matter.

Anna is right. It will matter. It will matter to them hugely that their own mother wrote it. Anna matters. Her story and her husband's story and their history matters. It is fun to know their children and to share in their joy at the births of their grandchildren. The future of those grandchildren, and all those as yet only in the mind of God, matters too. Anna is affirming that future grandly by tracing and writing her family histories.

Not everyone will be so determined. For those who find the idea of collecting stories, writing letters, making phone calls and plane trips overwhelming or impossible, there are other ways to keep some kind of record of family history.

My friend Debbie has adopted a unique way to catalog her own family's current history, with Valentine letters that include photos of family and special events with brief descriptions. Many families keep a copy of their family Christmas letter for the same purpose. I keep these and copies of all our "we've moved" cards, and also party invitations that we've sent out to help catalog special occasions and transitions in our family's story.

Pray about it, think about it, and find *some* way to value your story and your unique history. Because you matter, those who came before you matter, and so do those who will come after you. Time separates generations from one another now, but it will not be so in eternity.

# Chapter 6

# *Letter Writing:*
# The Almost Lost Art

Sir, more than kisses, letters mingle souls.

For, thus friends absent speak.

> John Donne (c. 1572-1631)
> *Verse Letter to Sir Henry Wotton*

Is there anything in the art of personal writing so intimate, so powerful, so touching as a handwritten letter?

The art of letter writing is nearly lost in our technological society. Classic letter writing—by hand, on paper, with a pen—is almost an obsolete mode of communication between persons. It is more rare every day, every year, and it has become therefore more of a gift to cherish.

There are few families I know who invest much time or energy keeping in touch through letters. There are so many *other* ways to keep in touch now. With the ever-rising cost of mailing a little two-ounce note, and when it is faster and sometimes cheaper to phone, FAX or transmit e-mail, people figure, why not?

Indeed, why not? Using the technology *is* practical, it *is* cheaper, it *is* wonderful to hear the voice of your loved one over the phone. But what are we giving up? Why do I call letter writing an almost lost art?

I have received many phone calls from my parents in which to enjoy the sound of their voices. On the phone, we talk spontaneously about the children, the relatives, the weather, the happenings of the day. We get in touch. Telephone calls are about immediacy.

I have also received many letters from my mother, all of which I have saved. When they arrive in the mail and I read them, I feel something more than "in touch." As hand-crafted items, they took time to create and they take time to appreciate. I linger over them with a cup of tea. They are typically newsy, but more; thoughtful, reflective, sometimes poignant and profound, and always filled with lovely phrases and a rich vocabulary. Letters—especially those my mother writes—are literary creations, and literature is about the deep and lasting things of life.

I have two lovely hand-written letters and numerous birthday cards from my father, the latest letter complete with a personally-signed copy of his own published article! I cherish them. I may frame them. When I can no longer hear his voice over the phone, I will still have these letters from his hand. How many friends I know who have never received even *one*! I have a friend whose only letter from her father, ever, was his suicide note blaming her and her sister and mother for his choice. Can you imagine?! I hope to see my friend, Hope, again despite many years when we were not in touch with each other, and that hope has been inspired by—what else?—a Christmas letter that reestablished our connection.

Letters are addressed from one person to another. That is why we call them personal—they contain the thoughts and sentiments of daily life as well as the happenings that are part of the history of a person, and depending on which person, sometimes the family as well.

Saving letters of loved ones or friends thus becomes a form of history keeping. Those who want to create a family history without having to write one from scratch might want to collect the letters of parents and grandparents and select a few that best illustrate something of who they were. Saving the letters of children has the same value.

Because they take some time to write, personal handwritten letters by their very nature help us to be more reflective. They can produce significant insights into life and faith and even into our relationship with God, revealing his character and ours and the character of the relationship we have with him.

Collections of personal letters from writers known primarily for their more formal works often contain a feast of such insights, such as this morsel from C.S. Lewis:

> We can bear to be refused but not to be ignored. In other words, our faith can survive many refusals if they really are refusals and not disregards. The apparent stone will be bread to us if we believe that a Father's hand put it into ours, in mercy or in justice or even in rebuke. It is hard and bitter, yet it can be chewed and swallowed. But if, having prayed for our heart's desire and got it, we then became convinced that this was a mere accident— that providential designs which had only some quite different end just couldn't help throwing out this satisfaction for us as a by-product—then the apparent bread would become a stone. A pretty stone, perhaps, or even a precious stone. But not edible to the soul.[1]

Very few of us, of course, achieve the insight or flair in our best writing that Lewis seemed to manage effortlessly even when penning a personal letter. Perhaps there is some comfort in realizing that even as prodigious a writer as he struggled to keep up with his correspondence!

Dear Mary,
I have got your note. It finds me with as clear a conscience about correspondence as a not very methodical, nor leisured, man ever has. I am pretty sure I have written to you since I last heard from you. Let us, however, make a compact that, if we are both alive next year, whenever we write to one another it shall *not* be at Christmas time. That period is becoming a sort of nightmare to me—it means endless quill-driving![2]

I sometimes wonder if Lewis' generation was the last in which many men had any "conscience about correspondence"! Men, in the last two or three generations, have led the way in discontinuing writing personal letters, with the notable exception of military men during wartime or the exceptional lover. Perhaps they began to lose the heart for letter writing when they left the farm, in the same way that many of them lost the time or heart for reading stories to their children or talking with their wives after a hard day away from home at the office or factory. Industrialization and urbanization have dramatically affected social relationships throughout our culture, and perhaps letter writing as well.

Women have, to a large degree, joined men in the workplace. One can understand why women whose days are filled with writing business letters and processing documents might also be disinclined to write a personal letter.

We find other ways to communicate instead. My friends with kids in college use the telephone, or now e-mail, almost exclusively as their preferred mode of communicating with their kids away from home. They know that a written letter is highly unlikely to ever receive a response in kind, and college students usually reflect vividly the general trends of broader society. In this regard, I am always heartened to hear a mother of a collegian say she has just sent off a care package with her son's favorite goodies and a big letter. It may be debatable which the young man might prefer more—the goodies or the letter—but there is no question that the sending of care packages is one of the last and best ways mothers continue to write a newsy letter that helps their kids away from home feel remembered and connected.

Who takes time to write a letter anymore?

Most of us moms don't bother anymore to see that our little children receive mail. What a joy we allow them to miss! People who live abroad and away from their families, whose children must learn to correspond with grandparents if they want some sense of the relationship, do a better job teaching their children the benefits of corresponding than we when our grandparents live just a few hours away.

I am grateful to my mother for her help, when our boys were younger, in sending small notes to them, often only two or three lines long, occasionally accompanied by a photo, a bookmark, a dollar, or a fun "coupon" that could be exchanged for a hug. Our boys, as a result, experienced the *fun* of receiving letters (though I did not do as well in helping them return them). I saw the fruit of my mother's creative investment when we lived abroad for awhile. The children all wrote a few letters and sent some tapes and photos to their friends, in part I think because they have experienced firsthand how meaningful it can be to receive something *personal* in the mail.

Generally, we tend to accept the decline in letter writing because of the alternative modes of communication available, but also because it seems so normal for people to be absorbed in the *here and now*. I understand. I am there myself. I do not write these thoughts because I have a clear conscience as a correspondent—rather, because I'd like to! I have dozens of dear friends to whom I would love to, even need to write. And do I do it? No, I am as absorbed in the here and now as much as anyone I know.

My mind tells me that the *"there and now"* is just as important as the here and now, and that my friends *there* matter just as much to me as my friends *here*. Most of us would say the same. But do we live like this is really true? I think most of us in Western society do not anymore.

American culture is absorbed with the here and now to the point of acting as though the there and now hardly matters. The difference is starkly evident in the newspapers of Europe as opposed to those of the U.S. By and large, European newspapers are weighted heavily with world news, covering a broad range of issues over a broad range of nations. American newspapers, by contrast, are parochial. Some of my European friends are honest enough to tell me that Americans are generally viewed with some disdain by Europeans on account of our provincialism. We seem (to them) to believe that "if it doesn't happen in America, it doesn't matter."

Add to this the increasing mobility of our society. The idea that friendships are meant to last for a lifetime seems hopelessly unrealistic to many. People move to take jobs, not to be with people they know. With every move, the number of people we got to know and then left behind increases. We might think that this would cause people to write more letters, but the effect is often just the opposite. People who move a lot (or who see a lot of friends come and go) may be less inclined to give their hearts deeply to new friendships, knowing that close relationships will only make it more painful to say good-bye. When it comes time to move on, we make vague promises to "stay in touch," but the short-term friendships that have been formed in one place are almost always left behind, and the idea of writing is barely considered.

I heard a woman describe this reality in her own life. Her husband's job required them to move every three to five years. She usually made one or two good friends in each place, but figured that in order to make room for new friends in the new place she would have to drop the "chore" of communicating with the others.

Perhaps the demise of personal letter writing in our society is symptomatic of how temporary and superficial our relationships have become.

At the risk of hypocrisy (for many of my friends have not seen a letter from me for quite a while!) I will raise a flag and a cheer for the classic, handwritten, personal letter! It is an art form worth preserving, and even more worth practicing, because letters of this kind are gifts of communication and signs of commitment in relationships.

Consider the word *correspondence*. As C.S. Lewis pointed out in his letter to Malcolm (quoted above), "We can bear to be refused but not to be ignored." Human beings are created for relationship and, as a result, we refuse to be ignored. Just ask the parents of any two-year-old! Put more positively, we thrive on being acknowledged. We need other humans who *respond* to us. Response validates our sense of self.

To respond to one another is what it means to be *correspondents*. "Co-respondents" are people who are mutually committed to responding to one another in written form. The dialogue they create together in letters becomes their *correspondence*.

Seen in this light, personal letter writing is not merely a means of self-expression, and certainly not a "chore" as though we must write letters as we write checks to pay what is owed. A personally written letter is a gift of one's self to another, a sign of mutual commitment in the relationship—an affirmation that the story we live (and write!) together matters.

My mother is one of the best examples I know of a person who has, for the better part of her life, been an excellent correspondent. My parents have moved enough times that she has collected a lot of friends. Remarkably, she has managed to keep in correspondence with many of them—most, in fact.

Mom typically has been a correspondent like my dear friend, Merrie Goddard, who nearly always manages to send me three or four letters for every one of mine to her! Mother and Merrie are both rare in the quantity of letters they produce. I must admit that, on my bad days, another letter in my mailbox has sometimes felt to me like another stone in my bucket of guilt and regret over not having responded as much as I want to.

Counting is a problem. We live in a tit-for-tat world: pay this, get that; get that, owe this. We too easily look at a personal letter as an invoice requesting payment, not a gift imparting grace.

Over time, I have learned from my mother and my friends that counting "letters received versus letters sent" was *my* problem, not theirs. Mom and Merrie write out of love for their friends, not with an eye to how many letters come back to them as compared with the number they send.

This is the nature of grace—the kind of love we all are given by God. Grace is not invoiced, not laden with tit-for-tat expectations, but given freely out of the fullness of the giver's heart. To give in this way is not "natural" to us, entrenched as we are in the give-and-get habits of our world—but it is God's way.

Jesus taught this way of loving and he also demonstrated it supremely. What is more, Jesus can be thought of as God's personal, handwritten letter to us, not piling on guilt but extending grace, acknowledging our value to him and God's commitment to us. As John the apostle puts it: "God did not send his Son into the world to condemn the world, but to save the world through him, (John 3:17)." In Jesus Christ, God invites us to correspond.

The number of letters sent or received is not a measure of the value of a person, the extent of our love, or the depth of commitment in a relationship. Christians would not rejoice more in the love of God if, somehow, God had sent *many* Sons "to save the world!" The fact that God sent his *only* Son is the wonder of The Story.

In the same way, I do not love my mother more for her many personal letters or my father less for his two. It is the fact of *who* wrote them, and that any are written at all, which makes them precious to me.

Letters are treasures on account of their writers, not the writers on account of their letters!

Having said all this, the problem remains for many of us that we have a hard time getting beyond our good intentions about corresponding to the actual doing of it.

What do I find helpful?

### Preparation

You will recognize this scenario: I go to the mailbox. A letter from a friend! I eagerly open it and read it with delight. She shares good news, or perhaps sadness. My heart is stirred to respond. I open the desk drawer in the kitchen to get a pen, but find only broken pencils. Some notebook paper hides under a pile of batteries and dried up marking pens, wrinkled and torn along the edges. This will never do! She has written on pretty stationery. I try another drawer and find the pad of plain white paper. At least it is unlined and letter-size. O.K. Now stamps. Are there any stamps? Phone books, scraps of paper, rubber bands, paper clips, and recipes as yet unfiled are pushed aside until I locate the little book of postage stamps at the back of the drawer. There is still one left! Yes! The phone rings, the kids need a ride, and my desire to write a brief, loving response is swept away in the daily tide. Noble impulses are often brought to a screeching halt by the smallest obstacles.

Life rushes too quickly for most of us to expect leisure for letter writing to be handed over without a struggle. A little preparation makes all the difference.

The desire to write is an impulse to respond to someone who matters to you, usually triggered by some thought of the person or by their last letter or phone call. The telephone serves these impulses because it is always ready, always nearby. Letter writing is really no less convenient, often can be less time-consuming, and is far less expensive (as compared with long-distance charges for that one hour visit!)—*if* you are prepared with the materials for writing.

Tomorrow, take a little shopping trip. For a small investment you can be fully equipped for correspondence!

Like my friend, Terry Glaspey, you may find it helpful to buy a supply of small notes and post cards that can be stamped ahead of time and do not require an envelope. Her philosophy: *send something that says you care and are thinking of the other person,* even if there is not a lot of time to write at length. Her system works. I have appreciated every card that Terry has sent me over the years.

I like to keep plenty of pretty stationery, lovely cards and note paper on hand. Different styles fit different moods—when I can afford to indulge my love of paper enough to have the ideal supply! I at least always manage to have that white unlined stationery-size pad on hand, so that if the pretty supply has run out, I have something that is minimally acceptable to write on. (My friends know that it is likely I cannot afford to keep up with my personal taste for stationery, and that it is more important to communicate and respond than to impress them with my taste!)

Postage stamps come in generic, plain and artistic styles—what matters most is to keep a good supply available. I try to plan for the bills that need stamps, as well as the letters and constant flow of thank you notes that leave the house. Happily, since the stamps are the same price whether pretty or plain, I can indulge taste preferences without guilt! Go for the pretty stamps—there are so many great choices!

I usually manage to have plenty of small, simple notes around for occasions when a "thank you" is needed. I try to anticipate the need and pick up some thank you cards routinely, and not just when I need them.

My favorite pen for writing letters is a fountain pen. Its ink flows easily and doesn't get "gummed up" like that of ball point pens, which also have the obnoxious habit of running out of ink in the middle of whatever you are writing. With my fountain pens (I have three: one for black, one for blue, and one for turquoise ink!) I can see when the ink is running low, and extra cartridges are inexpensive and easy to carry with me.

There is a tactile, even sensual, dimension to writing with a good pen on quality paper that suits the intimate nature of personal correspondence. I have not yet seen an e-mail message or fax that came scented with perfume, or nested a tiny, pressed flower, or held a tea-bag or bookmark—simple gifts that say I love you, or I care.

## Place

I dream of a beautiful writing desk by a window with a view, uncluttered by junk mail, bills, endless requests for charitable giving and newsletters. The idyllic picture in my mind is a cherry wood Queen Anne desk with drawers dedicated to my journal, my poetry, and my correspondence with friends.

That vision awaits fulfillment, but in the meantime the best "place" for my correspondence is portable. With active teenage students, a husband whose work involves endless books and paper documents, and all my various writing projects, we play a "musical chairs" game of sharing work space in our home. There is no horizontal surface that remains pristine or private for long.

Part of my dream has been realized, thanks to my husband's generosity and ingenuity. He has created a larger work space in our family room that allows me my own place for my freelance writing. I keep this space totally separate from my journal, poetry and personal correspondence. It is important to me to separate work from pleasure. Though I have pleasure in my work, it is still work.

The portable place for my correspondence stash is a large African grass bag that I can keep at hand, and that travels to the kitchen table, the dining room table, downstairs to the coffee table or upstairs again next to my bed. The bag does not travel all the time, but whenever I think I will take the time to respond to one letter, usually with a "tea break," I move it to where my body is most likely to be for an hour or so.

The bag holds my stationery and note cards, envelopes, pens, and some stamps (that are set aside *just* for correspondence—I'm a bit jealous that the pretty ones don't go for the bills!) and the letter or two that are most important to respond to first.

*Prompting*
What is it that prompts you out of that vague sense of "I should" into the focused decision of "I will"?

When a letter from a friend arrives in the mail, do you feel the impulse to respond right away, or is it easy to set it aside thinking that you will get to it later?

Again, you know the scenario. Inevitably, other tasks, seemingly more urgent, intrude on the impulse to respond immediately.

When I am very busy but *must* respond to a letter immediately, I use the phone. If the other person is not there but has an answering machine, I leave a quick, warm message of love and gratitude for the letter and try to make a quick response to something of what was written before the tape clicks off. This frees me from that vague sense of guilt that can creep in and allows me to put another more urgent letter first that has been waiting for awhile.

But when we set a letter aside, days go by. Good intentions to respond decay into guilt feelings we'd rather not acknowledge until, one day, digging back into our papers like an archaeologist, we excavate the letter from a deep layer of sediment and reacquaint ourselves with its now-ancient origins! Then we are faced with what may be the would-be-letter-writer's greatest obstacle: the guilt or embarrassment over how *much* time has lapsed since our friend's letter came!

Now it is impossible to respond to what was said as if it is still current news. Now we feel we should apologize and know it won't help. No one likes to receive an apology for our taking so long to respond. It tends to diminish the receiver of the apology as if he or she were sitting around, counting the weeks, or had no understanding or ability to identify with a full daily life! Nor do we like to justify ourselves, least of all by that horrid phrase, "I've been busy."

It's true of course. Everyone is busy. The person who sent you the letter, and who will be on the receiving side when you send your next letter, understands, and usually can identify. So much for the joy of personal correspondence? No. So much for the mistaken sense of guilt.

We would do better to remember that the person who sent that letter loves us.

How do you judge when it is time to answer a letter? For me, it is rather subjective, but I try to be organized and prioritize. I first separate my letters according to U.S. and international piles—I have a lot of correspondence with friends in Europe and Canada. I write on the envelopes "Received: Date." Then, particularly if they all have been sitting unresponded to, I reread them—skimming—and decide who I most *want* to respond to first.

The key here is the word *want*—no guilt. Do you enjoy receiving a letter from someone who feels motivated by guilt to write to you? I don't. Guilt-based relationships are no fun, in person, or in correspondence! So I work to not let guilt prompt me to respond. I want to respond from love when I genuinely can make the time to give expression to the love I have for the person.

My decision then, of whom I want to respond to first may be based on my sense of the other person's loneliness or need of a more timely response. I want to quickly send the message that I care at such times. More likely though, I choose to respond first to the correspondents with whom *I* feel most urgent about communicating something of my story at the time.

Allowing yourself to be prompted by your own desire to share your heart with someone you love is a wonderfully guilt-free way to communicate. The positive prompting of your heart to share yourself, which is always a gift, takes away the felt need to apologize for the great lapse of time between your friend's last letter and your response. Trusting that your correspondent already knows you enough to understand that you will respond when you can helps relieve unnecessary guilt when letters pile up.

Many times the Holy Spirit has put a friend on my mind to write to, someone who especially needed a caring letter when I otherwise had no reason to know it. Other times a letter from a friend has arrived in my mailbox on just the day I needed a lift, or needed to be reminded that others care about me. The Lord's timing is perfect.

For those who find journaling helpful, as discussed earlier, the reflections recorded in your journal could easily flow into a simple prayer that the Spirit would bring to your mind the friend to whom you should write next. It is uncanny how these simple prayers open us up to God's direction.

But what if you have someone you are actually *getting to know* by correspondence—someone you have spent very little time with face to face, or perhaps never met in person? Someone who may not yet have developed a history of trust and love in relationship with you, but is willing to treat you lovingly, because he or she is big-hearted and open-minded?

This an unusual form of correspondence in today's world, perhaps, but it exists. Writers and authors—who come to be "known" to some degree by their published works— have many such relationships I'm told, if they are willing to respond to the numerous people who want to know them (indeed, feel as if they *do* know them from their writings).

I have a dear corresponding friend whom I have not yet met in person, though I hope to soon. We do not know each other well yet, but we are working on it. She does not know that I *will* eventually get around to responding to her from my heart. I have already sensed that this is her way, too, and that we may share many common values and perhaps a few common dreams. I didn't foresee that it would be so long before we could meet. I hope that the trust and love that makes correspondence such a pleasure may be gained in time. I feel that her response to me— without knowing me well at all—is total grace. It matters to me to have someone affirm that my story matters too.

What about the letters that are a slower (not lower) priority?

I set goals.

### Goals
I write the date by which I want to respond on the envelope, under the date the letter was received. "Respond by: Date." Sometimes, I tell myself to "Respond this month!" I may not, and often don't make my own time-goal, but I usually get the letter responded to faster than when I just let it sit in a pile of forlorn letters that begin to seem unloved, as if the people who wrote them were too.

Once I had been freed from performance-orientation in friendship, which was motivated by guilt to "maintain" and "control" the relationship like a fire that would certainly go out if I didn't put wood on it constantly, I have found it much more pleasant to be grace-based in friendships both in person and on paper! It is unpleasant to go back to a sense that what you do is more important than who you are.

## Grace

I am eager to respond to my correspondents with grace. Their letters, no matter how old, are gifts of love to me, even when I set them aside so long that the news they shared is no longer new. I don't guilt myself over failing to respond in a timely manner to news. It may still warrant some acknowledgment as old news, when I am very late in responding, but I make it a priority to respond to the person first and to the specific statements of his or her outdated letter secondarily.

Listen for the heart feelings that are reflected between the lines of letters. The person can be known there, sometimes, more than in what they have actually written.

Don't decide that letters which have sat around for a few months are not worth rereading and trying to understand. Listen for the reflective tone, the thoughts that your correspondent has about life and truth—these are timeless things that can be responded to at any time.

As correspondents we may not always be prompt, but if we have the heart to treat our corresponding friends with freedom, grace and trust we will enjoy those qualities and find that we write when the time is right!

## Purpose

A sense of purpose in a relationship and why it matters to communicate makes a big difference in my motivation to respond, regardless of timeliness. I have already addressed several of those purposes: letters express love, convey friendship, communicate caring. Personal correspondence creates a dialogue, builds a relationship, records a story, and can even make close friends of people who have never met face to face. All of these are worthwhile purposes. Here are two more that I feel are of special importance.

First, personal letters may serve the purpose of helping to heal relationships that have become strained or broken.

I am sure you do not need to be told how often there is alienation in families and between friends, nor how painful these situations can be. Sometimes all our best efforts to talk and resolve difficult relationships do not succeed. Sometimes we make them worse by what we say. Sometimes people are unwilling even to talk to one another.

A thoughtful, well-written personal letter is sometimes the only recourse we have left, and it can be an effective tool of reconciliation—provided it is used as an instrument for healing and not for further alienation. Specifically, there are two types of letters which are almost always helpful and not hurtful.

The most important is the letter that says "I'm sorry." If I truly am sorry, I shouldn't let my pride keep me from saying so. If I don't think that a problem is all my fault, it still might be partly my fault and I can say I'm sorry for that. Even if I don't think that a problem is my fault *at all*, I can be sorry for what has happened in the relationship and for the alienation that has occurred. There are countless ways to helpfully and truthfully say "I'm sorry," and only one way to refuse.

Be careful, though, of the temptation to sneak in a verbal punch or two. An apology barbed with blame and recrimination is no apology at all. If you care about making things better, give up the "blame game" and simply say you're sorry.

The second most important letter for healing broken relationships is the unmailed letter.

Prose from an unmailed letter—

I can try to put myself into a neat little pile
of words, and set them before you
and hope you will be able to read into them
what I can't seem to express.
Perhaps there are two "Me's"
maybe more,
but the fact remains
they are all part of *me*.
I'm just *beginning* to discover which
are parts I *want* to be.

> Suzi Bert
> Fresno, 1968

Several times over the years I have found letter writing useful for expressing feelings that I had no intention of saying directly to another person, yet had to "get out" somehow. In the same way that journaling can be a sheltered place for dealing with strong emotions, the unmailed letter can be a way to begin to express anger, hurt or pain and to deal with the blame that we feel towards a particular person.

The unmailed letter becomes a tool for exploring what we feel and for clarifying what we really want to say and *choose* to say to the person. An unmailed letter gives time for assessing the realism of our expectations in the relationship. Often our anger and disappointment with others is caused by our own (perhaps unconscious) expectations of them, rather than their errant intention toward us. Writing out our anger or hurt—which reveals that our expectations have been disappointed—can help us get beyond blaming to prepare for a reconciliation. Through rehearsing our thoughts and feelings on paper, we may gather quiet strength for a necessary confrontation.

Such letters may be addressed to another person, but they are really written for the sake of the writer.

I am not advocating dishonesty here. In all relationships there are times of misunderstanding and hurtfulness. Honesty does not require that we give vent to every thought and emotion that happens to pass through our hearts. We do ourselves and the other person a favor to try to sort through the emotions that tumble inside us before we communicate again. The unsent letter is not to avoid communication, but to enhance it. Some of the most important letters I ever wrote were the ones I never sent!

There is one more purpose that personal letter writing may serve which is especially important to me as a Christian, and which may provide food for thought for you whether or not you are.

This purpose is illustrated by the a large portion of the New Testament which is composed of personal letters. They were written by Christian apostles like Paul and Peter and John, and were addressed to groups of believers or, in some cases, to individuals in the first century, A.D. They reflect the customary form of letters from that era and bear all the marks of authentic correspondence between friends who dearly loved each other.

These biblical letters, sometimes called epistles, are part of the bedrock foundation on which the Church has taken its stand to proclaim the Good News of salvation in Jesus Christ for nearly two thousand years. These letters tell a story. They preserve a history. They reveal the thinking, the emotions, the joys and the struggles of the men and women who knew Jesus Christ face-to-face and who became willing, in large numbers, to lay down their lives as witnesses for him.

Implicitly, these letters tell us something else—that the God revealed in the Bible uses real people like you and me, and normal modes of communication like personal letters, to pass along the most important message ever sent and the greatest story every told. I like to write my letters with the purpose of giving some reflection of God's love and good news to the receiver.

Do our letters matter? I have just received from my aunt a box of my father's letters written to his parents and sister when he was in the service during World War II. These are treasures to me, waiting to be discovered! I feel sure my father wrote any good news he could tell his family to reassure them of his health and safety.

Of course our letters matter to the recipient. Even though ours do not the carry same authority as the epistles of Scripture, the *same Spirit* who inspired Peter and Paul and John also prompts us to write encouragement and hope to a friend, or words of reconciliation to a friend we've lost. Our letters need not share the unique authority of the biblical letters to impart love and grace. It is the same Lord who preserved the text of sacred Scripture for generation after generation, through centuries and millennia, who can preserve the good we do through the letters we write.

Letter writing takes on its greatest significance when we recognize that we and others are part of something larger than ourselves. God has made clear his purpose of redeeming our troubled world. His work reached its climactic point in the life, death and resurrection of Jesus Christ, and now, while we await the consummation in his return, we have the opportunity to pass on through our letters a little bit of his love, his grace, a little story from our own lives of answered prayer and of witness to his faithfulness and personal care.

A weaver's shuttle, ferrying threads of many colors back and forth across the loom, gradually builds a fabric of exquisite beauty and strength—the "warp and woof" intertwined to make something entirely new that is greater than the individual threads which comprise it. Could it be that, from God's perspective, our personal correspondence—personal letters sent back and forth ferrying messages of friendship and encouragement and love—are likewise weaving a tapestry whose beauty we can now only glimpse, but which will one day be revealed in full?

How shall God's redemptive love affect our corresponding relationships with those we love who are near and those who are far away? How shall it affect our relationships with those who are alienated, who have hurt us or been hurt by us? Could a personal letter make an eternal difference?

Giving the gift of a letter is one way to say that the here and now, with all its "tyranny of the urgent," is not all that matters to us. Christ matters incalculably, and relationships with others matter because we are on a journey which, through Christ, leads to the eternal glory of his Kingdom.

How wonderful it would be if future generations might one day come across your personal correspondence and say, *"How they loved one another!"*

You matter. Your story matters. Your friends nearby and far away matter, and their stories matter. Where we all are going together matters, too. What we do to treasure each other along the way matters.

Write a letter. Send a thank you note. Say you're sorry. Start a dialogue in written form. Respond. Communicate! We are writing the story of our lives.

# End Notes

### Introduction
1 Ted Koppel, "Media Courtesans," *Harpers*, January, 1986, (New York, New York: Harpers Magazine Foundation), p. 18.

### Chapter One
1 Mona Brooks, *Drawing with Children* (Los Angeles, California: Jeremy P. Tarcher, Inc., 1986), pp. xix-xxii.

### Chapter Two
1 Dan Allender and Tremper Longman, *Cry of the Soul* (Colorado Springs, Colorado: NavPress Publishing Group, 1994), p. 17.
2 Luci Shaw, *Life Path: Personal and Spiritual Growth Through Journal Writing* (Portland, Oregon: Multnomah Press, 1991), p. 78.

### Chapter Three
1 William B. Yeats, *The Collected Works of W.B. Yeats: the Poems, Vol. 1* (New York, New York: MacMillan, 1983), Sonnet No. 74, p. 73.
2 G.K. Chesterton, "On Poetry," *Radix* Magazine, Volume 22 Number 2, (*Radix* Magazine, Inc.), p. 31.
3 Emily Dickinson, *Bolts of Melody: New Poems of Emily Dickinson*, edited by Todd and Bingham (New York, New York: Harper and Brothers, 1945), p. 233.
4 Charles Darwin, *Autobiography*, as quoted by Virginia Stem Owens, "Seeing Christianity in Red and Green as Well as Black and White," *Christianity Today*, Sept. 2, 1983 (Carol Stream, Illinois: Christianity Today, Inc.), p. 38.
5 Madeleine L'Engle, from *A Wrinkle in Time*, as quoted by Catherine Calvert in "A Gift for Magic and Truth," *Victoria* Magazine, Vol. 9 #1, Jan. 1995 (New York, New York: Hearst Magazines), p. 29.

6 Mark Noll, *A Widening Light: Poems of the Incarnation*, edited by Luci Shaw (Vancouver, B.C.: Regent College Bookstore, 1994), p. 118.

7 Walt Whitman, "Song of Myself," *Leaves of Grass* (New York, New York: Modern Library, 1940), pp. 71-72.

8 Natalie Goldberg , *Writing Down the Bones: Freeing the Writer Within* (Boston, Massachusetts: Shambala, 1986), pp. 32-33.

**Chapter Four**

1 Ernest Hemingway, *Selected Letters: 1917-1961*, edited by Carlos Baker (New York, New York: Charles Scribner and Sons, 1981), pp. 800-801.

2 Henri Nouwen, *Genesee Diary* (Garden City, New York: Image Books, Doubleday and Co., Inc., 1981), p. 121.

3 Madeleine L'Engle, *Walking on Water: Reflections on Faith & Art* (Wheaton, Illinois: Harold Shaw Publishers), pp. 41, 44.

4 Ibid., p. 143.

5 Ibid., p. 193.

6 Margery Williams, *The Velveteen Rabbit* (Garden City, New York: Doubleday, 1971), p. 20.

7 Phyllis A. Whitney, *Guide to Fiction Writing* (Boston, Massachusetts: The Writer, Inc., 1982)

**Chapter Five**

1 Madeleine L'Engle, "Story as the Search for Truth," *Radix* Magazine, Volume 22 Number 2 (Berkeley, California: Radix Magazine, Inc.), p. 10.

**Chapter Six**

1 C.S. Lewis, *Letters to Malcolm: Chiefly on Prayer* (New York, New York: Harcourt Brace Jovanovich, Publishers, 1964), p. 53.

2 C.S. Lewis, *Letters to An American Lady* (New York, New York: Pyramid Books, William B. Eerdmans Publishing Co., 1971), p. 88.

# Acknowledgments

Man is not only a contributory creature,
but a total creature; he does not only make one,
but he is all; he is not a piece of the world,
but the world itself; and next to the glory of God,
the reason why there is a world.

John Donne
*Sermons*

I acknowledge with heartfelt thanks my friends and family members who have contributed to this book. Thank you for sharing your stories and friendship with me. Without you, it would have been too much of me and not a reflection of the variety, creativity and devotion to God that illustrates my message—each of your stories matters to me.

Karen Adams, for thorough proofreading of the second edition.

Cindy Bennett, for her *pensées* and a new prayer partnership across cultures.

Hazel Bert, for her mantle of prayer, and for praying.

Marylou Bert, for three poems, many wonderful letters, loving encouragement, and a great childhood of stories and poetry and fun.

Orville E. Bert, for information on his grandmother Susan, Grandpa's poem, his loving letters, laughter and a rich heritage of grace, support and prayer.

Ashlie Fletcher, for her poem, and for inspiring Noel to go to Albania.

Debbie Fletcher, for her journal entry and a long special friendship.

Julie Gephart, for her journal entry and ten years of lovely prayer partnership.

Jeannette Clift George, for her kind comments and encouragement in the love of the arts.

Margie Gilchrist, for her journal entry and a precious, always current friendship, and for widely distributing the second edition.

Merrie Goddard, for her journal entry, a *pensée* and enduring multi-dimensional friendship.

Isabelle Goddard, for her journal entry, mentoring, visionary communications, and enduring loyal friendship.

Marcie Jacques, for the beautiful cover design, title and chapter pages, and the gift of her artistic support.

Sarah Meekhof, for her journaling-for-the-children vision, the excerpt from her children's story, and a delightful writing friendship.

Kathleen Moore, for her synthesis of an arduous journey of love through "attachment therapy," and keeping our friendship.

Judy Palpant, for more entries than I had space for, empathy, and great encouragement.

Bob Paul, for affirmation of my thoughts, editing, formatting, and a loving partnership in marriage and ministry.

Noel Paul, for his poem, and for being a great person as well as a son I delight in.

Alex and Aaron Paul, for getting their own meals and joking good-naturedly about Mom's being stuck to the computer.

Eugene Peterson, for his excellent endorsement of my message and encouragement of my studies and stories.

Sam Reeves, for his visionary influence, long supportive friendship, and powerful comments about my writing.

Douglas Rumford, for his advocacy of me as a writer, and his great endorsement.

Glenda Schlahta, for thoughtful, editing of the third edition and shared joy in books and authors.

Luci Shaw, for her lovely endorsement, helpful suggestions, and her encouragement to me as a writer.

Barbara Helen Tompkins, for promoting my second edition widely, and for a sturdy friendship.

Anna & Alan Waltar, for their story of the two family histories and encouraging friendship.

Manya White, for her journal entry and an endearing friendship.

Martha Zimmerman, for her journal entry and her affirmation of my writing.

# Glossary

Below are selected definitions from *Webster's II New College Dictionary*, published by the Houghton Mifflin Company in 1995. Additional meanings for these terms, according to my experience of current usage, are italicized.

**Creative Writing**—gerund (functioning as a noun):
Creative—adj.: "1) Having the power or ability to create; 2) Productive; 3) Marked by originality; Imaginative."
Writing—noun: "3) A written work, esp. a literary composition."

*Imaginative or original writings; a written art form; an umbrella term for all written work produced for personal expression, human interest, academic assignment or art.*

**Diary**—noun: "1) A daily record; 2) A book for keeping a diary."

*An empty book with line pages, usually one page per day and numbered for one year, often with lock and key; Affords some privacy, but not conducive to reflection or creative writing.*

**Genre**—noun: "1) Type: class; 2)a) An artistic category marked by a distinctive style, form, or content; b) A distinctive category of literary composition."

**Journal**—noun: "1)a) A personal record of experiences kept on a regular basis; b) A record of daily events; 2) A daybook."

*An empty book with or without lines, usually without days or dates denoted, for one to write and/or draw in for any purpose desired; A book kept for personal and reflective purpose; Specialized journals focus on a particular theme (e.g. gardening, children, travel, holiday and parental memories, etc.).*

**Journal**—*verb: To write in a journal; To make written entries on a periodic or regular basis, or during particular seasons of life (e.g. crises, vacations, trips, holidays. etc.).*

**Journaler**—*noun: One who journals, esp. one who keeps a personal journal.*

**Journaling**—*verb: The ongoing action of writing in a journal.*

**Journalist**—noun: "1) One whose occupation is journalism; 2) One who keeps a journal."

*The second definition is still correct and may still find usage esp. in the business world, but is largely outdated among reflective journalers, health care professionals, teachers and others who recommend journaling for creative purposes.*

**Journalize**—verb: "1) To record in a journal; 2) To keep a personal or financial record."

*Again, this is correct usage, but is mostly outdated except within the contexts of business, (e.g. keeping a daily financial log or a ship's log).*

**Letter**—noun: "1) Written communication directed to another."

*A personal correspondence written from one person to another.*

**Poem**—noun: "1) A composition designed to convey a vivid and imaginative experience by the use of condensed language chosen for its sound and suggestive power as well as for its meaning. . . and by the use of literary techniques as structured meter, natural cadences, rhyme or metaphor; 2) A composition in verse rather than prose."

*A composition in verse of intensity or beauty which may or may not have rhythmic meter or rhyme.*

**Poetic**—adj.: "1) Of or relating to poetry; 2) Having a quality or style characteristic of poetry."

**Poetry**—noun: "1) The art of a poet; 2) A division of literature; a) The poetic works of a given author, group or nation; 3) A composition written in meter; 4) prose resembling poetry in some respect, as in form or sound."

**Prose**—noun: "1) Ordinary speech in writing; 2) Commonplace expression or quality."

*Nearly everything sold in a bookstore in written form, except poetry; "Prose book" may connote a collection of thoughts, quotes, small vignettes or stories (truth or fiction), focused on a theme (e.g. love, wine, roses, romance, herbs, etc.).*

**Story**—noun: "1) Narration of an event or series of events; 2) A fictional prose or verse narrative intended to interest or amuse: Tale; 3) A short story; 4) The plot or narrative of a dramatic work; 5) A report, statement or allegation of facts; 6) A news article or broadcast; 7) An anecdote; 9) A legend or tradition."

*An umbrella term for a vast assortment of narratives, fiction and non-fiction; Often connotes fiction (e.g. fairy tale, short story, novel) in the context of creative story writing; A euphemism for a lie; A history of something, someplace or someone (e.g. biographical, national, religious, autobiographical, a family history, or a cultural myth or tradition.*

**Your story**—*noun: Your journey through life; If you write it: your personal history; Autobiography.*

# Select Bibliography

This bibliography is selected and divided for your convenience by subjects that have been considered in the text. I recommend them to budding writers and authors; they are all included in a growing book list that I offer in my writer's workshops. Since I have not addressed publishing in this book, those interested in publishing will find several books on the first list that do consider publishing questions. The quotes are included to inspire you to further exploration.

## On Reading and Writing

In matters of truth the fact that you don't want
to publish something is, nine times out of ten,
a proof that you ought to publish.

G.K. Chesterton
*A Miscellany of Men*

Appelbaum, Judith. *How To Get Happily Published.* New York, New York: Harper Perennial, 1992.

Bettelheim, Bruno. *The Uses of Enchantment: The Meaning and Importance of Fairy Tales.* New York, New York: Vintage Books, Random House, Inc., 1977.

Buechner, Frederick. *Telling the Truth: The Gospel as Tragedy, Comedy and Fairy Tale.* San Francisco, California: HarperSanFrancisco, 1977.

Coles, Robert. *The Call of Stories.* Boston, Massachusetts: Houghton Mifflin, 1989.

Dillard, Annie. *The Writing Life.* New York, New York: Harper Perennial, 1990.

_____. *Living by Fiction.* New York, New York: Perennial Library, Harper and Row Publishers, 1982.

Goldberg, Natalie. *Writing Down the Bones: Freeing the Writer Within.* Boston, Massachusetts: Shambhala Publications, Inc., 1986.

Holmes, Marjorie. *Writing Articles From the Heart: How to Write and Sell Your Life Experiences.* Cincinnati, Ohio: Writer's Digest Books, 1993.

Hunt, Gladys. *Honey For A Child's Heart.* Grand Rapids, Michigan: Zondervan Publishing House, 1978.

Lamont, Anne. *Bird by Bird: Some Instructions on Writing and Life.* New York, New York: Anchor Books, Doubleday, 1994.

L'Engle, Madeleine. *Walking on Water: Reflections on Faith and Art.* Wheaton, Illinois: Harold Shaw Publishers, 1972.

_____. "Story as the Search for Truth." *Radix Magazine,* Volume 22 No. 2, Berkeley, California: Radix Magazine, Inc. ,1996

Lindberg, Anne Morrow. *Gift from the Sea.* New York, New York: Random House, Inc., 1955.

Morris, Gilbert. *How to Write (and Sell) a Christian Novel.* Ann Arbor, Michigan: Vine Books, Servant Publications, 1994.

O'Connor, Flannery. "The Nature and Aim of Fiction,"
*Mystery and Manners*. ed. Sally and Robert Fitzgerald.
New York, New York: Farrar, Straus and Giroux, 1969.

Paterson, Katherine. *The Spying Heart: More Thoughts
on Reading and Writing for Children*. New York:
Lodestar Books, E.P. Dutton, 1989.

Phillips, Larry W., ed. *Ernest Hemingway On Writing*.
New York, New York: Charles Scribner's Sons, 1984.

Rilke, Rainer Maria. *Letters to a Young Poet*. New York,
New York: Vintage Books, Random House, Inc. 1986.

Seuling, Barbara. *How to Write a Children's Book and Get It
Published*. New York, New York: Charles Scribner's
Sons, 1991.

Shaughnessy, Susan. *Walking on Alligators*. San Francisco,
California: HarperSanFrancisco, 1993.

Stanek, Lou Willett. *So You Want to Write a Novel*. New
York, New York: Avon Books, 1994.

Stoddard, Alexandra. *The Gift of a Letter*. New York, New
York: Avon Books, 1990.

Ueland, Brenda. *If You Want To Write: A Book About Art,
Independence and Spirit*. St. Paul, Minnesota: Graywolf
Press, 1987.

Whitney, Phyllis A. *Guide to Fiction Writing*. Boston,
Massachusetts: The Writer, Inc., 1982.

Yancey, Philip. *Open Windows*. Westchester, Illinois:
Crossway Books, Good News Publishers, 1982.

# On Personal and Spiritual Growth and Journal-keeping

It has been said that when human beings stop
believing in God they believe nothing. The truth
is much worse: they believe in anything.

Malcom Muggeridge
*Tread Softly for You Tread on
My Jokes*

Allender, Dan B., and Longman, Tremper. *The Cry of the
Soul: How Our Emotions Reveal Our Deepest Questions
about God.* Colorado Springs, Colorado: NavPress
Publishing Group, 1994.

Blackaby, Henry and King, Claude. *Experiencing God.*
Nashville, Tennessee: Broadman and Holman
Publishers, 1994.

Bonhoeffer, Dietrich. *Life Together.* New York, New York:
Harper and Row Publishers, 1954.

Buechner, Frederick. *The Alphabet of Grace.* San
Francisco, California: HarperSanFrancisco, 1970.

_____. *Wishful Thinking: A Seeker's ABC.* San
Francisco, California: HarperSanFrancisco, 1973.

_____. *Sacred Journey.* San Francisco, California:
HarperSanFranciso, 1982.

Fee, Gordon D., and Stuart, Douglas. *How to Read the Bible for All Its Worth.* Grand Rapids, Michigan: Zondervan Publishing House, 1993.

Foster, Richard. *Celebration of Discipline.* New York, New York: Harper and Row Publishers, 1988.

L'Engle, Madeleine. *A Rock That is Higher: Story as Truth.* Wheaton, Illinois: Harold Shaw Publishers, 1993.

Lindberg, Anne Morrow. *Bring Me a Unicorn.* New York, New York: Signet Books, The New American Library, 1973.

MacDonald, George. *Diary of an Old Soul.* Minneapolis, Minnesota: Augsburg Fortress, 1994.

Merton, Thomas. *Thoughts in Solitude.* New York, New York: The Noonday Press, Farrar, Straus and Giroux, 1956.

Moore, Thomas. *Care of the Soul: A Guide for Cultivating Depth and Sacredness in Everyday Life.* New York, New York: HarperCollins Publishers, 1992.

Nouwen, Henri. *The Genessee Diary: Report from a Trappist Monastery.* Garden City, New York: Image Books, Doubleday, 1981.

_____. *Out of Solitude: Three Meditations on the Christian Life.* Notre Dame, Indiana: Ave Maria Press, 1974.

Owens, Virginia Stem. *If You Do Love Old Men.* Grand Rapids, Michigan: W. B. Eerdmans Publishing Company, 1990.

Peterson, Eugene H. *Spiritual Reading: An Annotated List.* Vancouver, B.C.: Regent College Bookstore Publication, 1989.

_____. *Subversive Spirituality.* Vancouver, B.C.: Regent College Bookstore Publication, 1994.

Postema, Don. *Space for God: A Study and Practice of Spirituality and Prayer.* Grand Rapids, Michigan: Christian Reformed Church Publications, 1983.

Rumford, Douglas J. *SoulShaping: Taking Care of Your Spiritual Life.* Wheaton, Illinois: Tyndale House Publishers, 1996.

Shaw, Luci. *Life Path: Personal and Spiritual Growth through Journal Writing.* Portland, Oregon: Multnomah Press, 1991.

_____. *God in the Dark.* Grand Rapids, Michigan: Broadmoor Books, Zondervan Publishing House, 1989.

Smalley, Gary, and Trent, John. *The Language of Love.* Pomona, California: Focus on the Family Publishing, 1988.

Smith, Margaret D. *Journal Keeper.* Grand Rapids, Michigan: W. B. Eerdmans Publishing Company, 1992.

Tournier, Paul. *The Gift of Feeling.* Atlanta, Georgia: John Knox Press, 1981.

Underhill, Evelyn. *Concerning Inner Life.* Rockport, Massachusetts: One World Publishing, 1995.

_____. *Fragments from an Inner Life: The Notebook of Evelyn Underhill.* ed. Dana Greene. Ridgefield, Connecticut: More House Publications, 1993.

Wakefield, Dan. *The Story of Your Life: Writing a Spiritual Autobiography.* Boston, Massachusetts: Beacon Press, 1990.

# Classic Christian Contemplatives

Talk to me about the truth of religion and I'll listen
gladly. Talk to me about the duty of religion and
I'll listen submissively. But don't come talking to
me about the consolations of religion or I shall
suspect that you don't understand.

C.S. Lewis
*The Unquiet Grave*

Aelred of Rievaulx. *Spiritual Friendship*. Kalamazoo,
Michigan: Cistercian Publications, 1977.

Brother Lawrence. *Practice of the Presence of God*.
Translated by Conrad DeMeester. Washington, D.C.:
Institute of Carmelite Studies Publications, 1994.

Ignatius of Loyola. *Spiritual Exercises*. Kalamazoo,
Michigan: Cistercian Publications, 1989.

Theresa of Avila. *The Interior Castle*. Translated by E.
Allison Piers. New York, New York: Image Books,
Doubleday, 1961.

Thomas à Kempis. *Imitation of Christ*. London, England:
Penguin Books, 1984.

Thomas R. Kelly. *A Testament of Devotion*. San Francisco,
California: HarperSanFrancisco, 1992.

St. Augustine. *Confessions*. Translated by Henry
Chadwick. Oxford, England: Oxford University Press,
1992.

St. John of the Cross. *Dark Night of the Soul*. New York,
New York: Image Books, Doubleday, 1990.